VANISHED HOUSES

OF SOUTH DEVON

Rosemary Lauder

LITTLECOURT TAVISTOCK. DEVON.

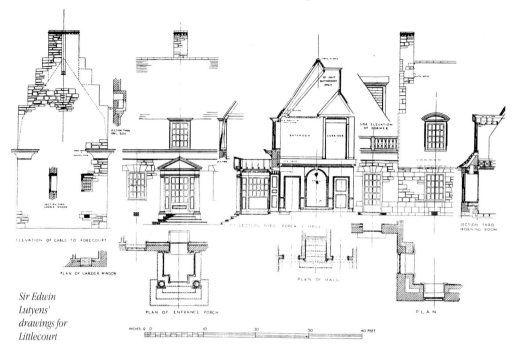

Sir Edwin Lutyens' drawings for Littlecourt

Many people have helped in the research for this book, and have been most generous in the loan of photographs and sales catalogues.

To them my grateful thanks, because without you this would have been a hopeless task. As it is, I have travelled all over the country in my quest for information, visiting Barings London headquarters just days before the dramatic crash. Much help has also come from librarians and Record Office staff. At times I have felt like a detective following up clues, and some questions remain unanswered, but to the best of my knowledge, everything is based on fact, and is accurate. Later facts may come to light that alter some aspects and no doubt someone will contact me after the book appears with some piece of missing information. I hope you get as much pleasure from reading this journey through history as I did from writing it.

Sources

Tristram Risdon, *Survey of Devon,* written 1605-30, published 1811
Rev Richard Polwhele, *History of Devonshire,* 1793-1806
Rev Daniel Lysons, *Magna Britannica,* 1822
Prof W G Hoskins, *Devon,* 1954

Typesetting and page make-up by ProFile (01392 841625)
Printing by Maslands Ltd (01884 252613)
Published 1997 by North Devon Books, Bideford, N Devon.

Front cover painting Lindridge by Felix Kelly (National Trust, photo Cliff Guttridge)
Back cover painting shows the interior of Haldon House in the 1900's

THE HOUSES...

Membland
...page 11

Lindridge ...page 36

Haldon
...page 48

Shobrooke ...page 67

Marley ...page 78

Silverton ...page 93

Fowlescombe ...page 115

INTRODUCTION

THERE are many 'vanished' houses in Devon, some small, some ancient, some grandiose. Why these seven? Something of each remains, enough to stir the imagination, be it only a gatepost and an overgrown drive.

Membland Hall

Silence is always more profound where once there was noise and bustle …memories haunt the old outbuildings; ghosts of times past wander among the towering trees and lament at the loss of what was once a noble dwelling. Why were such houses built? Who were their owners – and why did they disappear? Only one, the oldest, survives as a ruin, allowed to crumble year by year, in a state of romantic desolation.

Two were destroyed by fire, Lindridge and Shobrooke, and the remaining four were demolished, and no doubt many a nearby building incorporates stone, timber, fireplaces etc from one of them.

Poor Marley has been completely built over, and although the lodge and some stable buildings survive, it is difficult to imagine the marble villa in its setting.

Lord Cable at Lindridge

The parkland at Shobrooke is as beautiful as ever it was in the heyday of the house. At Silverton all is deserted and peaceful, and the Landmark Trust has stepped in to save the stables.

Membland is a thriving community. All the outbuildings, which are more attractive than the house ever was, have been adapted into highly sought after dwellings. The lodges remain, the last completed only a year before the Baring disaster, and the ornate wrought iron gates with intertwined initials. But they no longer open onto well-kept drives; such gates and lodges are one of the saddest indicators of a lost house; pointless mementoes of past glory when the aristocracy, and even Royalty, would sweep through and on up the drive to arrive at the grand entrance front with a flourish. Now only pheasants and scuttling rabbits disturb the silence.

On the site of Lindridge, after many hiccups and changes of ownership, an even larger building has replaced the burnt out shell, and this and all the outbuildings are divided into luxury homes. The Italian gardens have been rescued and face a reasonably secure future, though never again will they be as elaborate as when Lord Cable posed on the island in the lilypond.

Haldon, too, has been much built on. The pleasure grounds survive in excellent condition, but completely separate, and what was left after the demolition sale is now in two parts, one a private house, and one the Lord Haldon Hotel. High on the skyline the Belvedere, recently restored by the Devon Historic Building Fund, looks down. The memorial to General Lawrence is an eye-catching landmark, whilst the Palk family have none. Not one statue or monument survives to record their considerable influence (and one-time wealth) in this corner of Devon. Nor are there any portraits or photographs. All the farms and cottages on the estate are well maintained and many of them bear the hallmarks of their former use and ownership. But of Haldon's glory only a very small site, and part of the basement walls, remain. It is a sad loss for, had Haldon survived, it would have been revered as a little-altered mansion of the mid 18th century, built in the foremost style of the time, and embellished only 50 years later by a man of considerable wealth with access to a marvellous source of timber. It must have been very beautiful.

It was trade that built Marley, that purchased Lindridge and Haldon, and that completely altered Membland. It was old-established wealth that was responsible for Silverton, although very hefty mortgages were required for the grandiose plans of its builder.

Before foreign markets were opened up, it was the legal profession that seemed to offer the best opportunity of accumulating wealth. Fowlescombe, Lindridge and Shobrooke were built by lawyers retiring from the London Courts with amazing fortunes. Foreign enterprises in the West Indies built up the wealth of Sir Peter Lear who greatly enhanced Lindridge, and Marley was built on guano riches. Robert Palk and Edward Cable were both nabobs with considerable Indian wealth to pay for their country estates.

These seven are not by any means the only losses in Devon, but they were in their day the most fashionable, the best examples of wealth and power, and although memories are fast fading, it has been possible to recreate a picture of them.

One of the largest houses ever to be built in Devon has vanished almost without trace. On the cliffs at Wembury rose a huge mansion, which in the 1674 Hearth Tax returns, when it was owned by the Duke of Albermarle, had a massive 42 hearths, around 20 more than anywhere else. But apart from one drawing and a brief description, only a few fragments of wall remain. The builder was an "eminent lawyer in the reigns of Queen Elizabeth and King James, who returned to his native Devon with a fortune of £100,000" writes Risdon. "Sir John Heale made a magnificent house equal if not exceeding any other in these western parts for uniformity of building – a sightly seat for show – for receipt spacious; for cost sumptious; for site salubrious…"

One description tells of a great hall built on the lines of a Roman temple, ascended by steps with

Wembury House

"rayls and balisters". The only information on its ending comes in Lysons who states that "Wembury was pulled down by Mr Lockyer who sold the materials for £800, and built a mansion on the site for himself." Old, wily Sir John, however, has the only lasting memorial; he died in 1608, aged 66 and is buried at Wembury.

Plymouth has engulfed the site of Radford, ancient seat of the ancient Harris family. When it was built it would have been deep in the country. The earliest mention of Radford is in 1206; the house is described as Elizabethan, and its first owner of note was Sir Christopher Harris, MP for Plymouth, contemporary and friend of Sir Francis Drake. It is said he kept Sir Walter Raleigh prisoner at Radford in 1618.

A full description of the house as it was prior to its demolition in 1937, comes from Mr G Copeland in the *Transactions* of the Devonshire Association for 1945. He describes a house much altered over the centuries, given a grander front as fashions and fortunes changed.

> *The central block and north-east wing had prominent moulded eaves cornices on their outer faces, and higher-pitched roofs, the ridge of the north-east roof being somewhat lower than that of the central block, and hipped. The chimney-stacks at this end were numerous, lofty, rectangular, and of brick, their sides decorated each with a single blind arch. The stack at the north-east rose from a prominent stone breast, and like the others seemed to be of the late 17th century. The windows were similar, but those of the central block had prominent double keystones, and all had lightly moulded bars.*

The rear, he tells us, retained its early outline, with a small inner court with a wooden colonnade supporting projecting slate-hung upper storeys. The interior was full of panelling and moulding, with an ornate 16th century chimneypiece in the dining room, featuring caryatids, and a frieze of heraldic shields, which Mr Copeland supposes were all stolen whilst the house stood empty.

> *The Harris family retained Radstock until recent times, when it passed to the Bulteels, and to a Mr Mitchell, who was the last owner. Some representations were made locally to try to preserve the house from demolition, but the state of dilapidation into which this mansion of 50 rooms was slowly but surely falling, and the ever-increasing expenditure ... sealed its fate in favour of a controllable building estate. The most important of the interior fittings were put up for sale, and the work of demolition was so thoroughly carried out that not a fragment remains standing on the original site of the house. Apart from the 'ruins' on the site of the lake, our only reminders of Radford as a house are a pair of small dwarf octagonal gatepiers with ball finials adjoining a small square 18th century lodge, with a triangular pediment to each face and a small circular 'dome' not unlike the lid of a sweet bottle, at the end of a long disused carriage drive on the road to Deans Cross.*

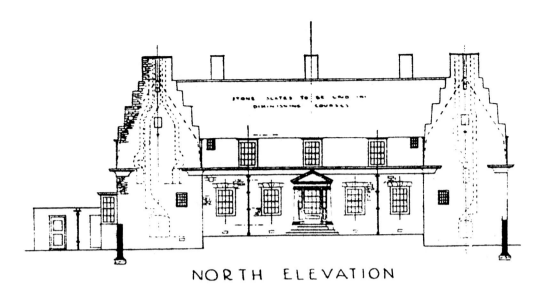

NORTH ELEVATION

Partially destroyed by fire in 1935 was one of the County's few examples of the work of Sir Edwin Lutyens. Littlecourt, on the outskirts of Tavistock, was built on land sold by the Bedford Estates, close to the golf course and planned for a few, select substantial houses. Littlecourt was one such, approached via a reasonable length of drive, with sundry outbuildings and a distinctive Lutyens appearance which included a steeply pitched roof. This was destroyed along with most of the upper storey, and Littlecourt survives today as a single storey residence. A *Country Life* article of 1925 records the interiors, and a sale catalogue of 1922 shows the property as it was before the fire. The setting has recently been completely ruined by the sale of the grounds for building.

Sir Edwin Lutyens' drawings for Littlecourt

Oldstone, near Dartmouth

Oldstone, near Dartmouth, is another sad loss of a small manor house, destroyed by fire in 1893, and recorded in a small book by a descendant of the last owners, the Dimes.

Another enormous house that is now reduced to farmhouse size is Heanton Satchville, near Merton. It noted 14 hearths in the 1668 Hearth Tax returns. Polwhele, writing at the end of the 18th century described it "Heanton House, a mansion built in the form of a letter E whence it referred to the days of Elizabeth. It occupies a large plot of ground but presents nothing remarkable in the point of architecture. In Col Rolles' and Lord Orford's time it was a place of good resort and a motto carved in wood in the dining parlour reminds us of those convivial days: 'He that sits down first gives least trouble.'"

The Rev Lysons, writing in 1822, tells us that "the estate had passed down through several families since the Sackvilles owned it in the time of Richard I, and passed eventually to the Rolles of Stevenstone,

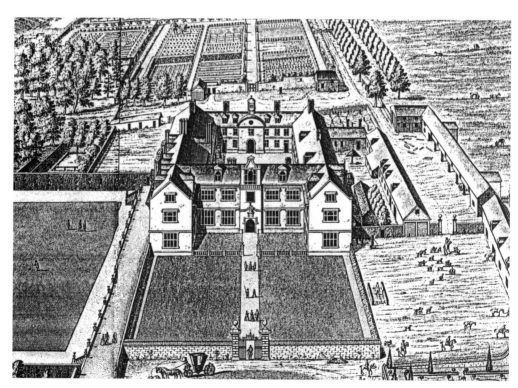

Heanton Satchville

a daughter of whom married Robert Walpole, Earl of Orford. In 1791 the barony of Clinton and estate passed to George Trefusis. …Heanton Satchville, which was some time seat of the Rolles and afterwards Earls of Orford, was burnt down several years ago – a farmhouse has been fitted out of the ruins. The deerpark is still kept up."

Creedy Park

Fire also destroyed the original Creedy House, close to Shobrooke, although this has been rebuilt.

Creedy, the seat of Sir John Davie Bt, scion of the old stock, near Bideford. One of the four sons of Mr Davie settled near Crediton where he was thrice Mayor and acquired considerable wealth. About the beginning of the last century he built Newhouse, since more properly called Creedy because of its vicinity to the river. A descendant of this gentleman was created baronet in 1641 and his posterity in lineal succession have made this seat their place of residence to the present baronet, Sir John Davie. The house has during so long a space in all probability undergone material alterations for its present appearance consisting of two handsome fronts cannot be referred to the style of architecture subsisting at the end of Elizabeth's or the beginning of James' 1st reigns. The two projecting wings in front indeed savour somewhat of the period and notwithstanding the guise of modern fashion may have been a portion of the original fabric. The situation of Creedy Park is fine surrounded by what was a park but which had been converted by the late baronet who was a great practical agriculturalist into pasture grounds. He had surrounded the whole with a wall at vast expense which rendered the grounds more compact and less liable to being trespassed on but did not add to the picturesque. (Rev John Swete)

The common thread running through the demise of all these houses is the loss of wealth, and the loss of status of their owners.

Such houses belonged to another age, an age of stability, of hereditary wealth and land ownership. New wealth, made in a less gentlemanly way, sought to buy its way into the landed aristocracy. As the centuries old base was gradually eroded, so was the ability of the owners to maintain their properties. It is a common link that not one of these houses could find a purchaser interested in living in them as a home, or even an hotel. Despite all the up-to-date equipment, and its modern design and construction, not even Marley succeeded.

In four cases the sharks stepped in, either in the form of a timber merchant (Lindridge and Haldon), or a developer. Only Shobrooke remains an entity because it is still owned by the same family. But had the house not been burnt down, it might have been a different story, and here too, the parkland might have been denuded of its glorious trees and been covered with neat executive homes.

The exigencies of the First World War put paid to any hope there might have been. At Haldon and Lindridge the only sons were killed. Both houses found use as hospitals, and Membland was a training base.

Silverton was already razed to the ground, and Fowlescombe empty and derelict.

Although the owners of Marley were wealthy enough to have other houses in which they preferred to live, their money was not based on land and there was no supporting estate with the house. Their incredible wealth did not survive to maintain an unwanted home, and their cosmopolitan blood took them away from damp and drizzling England.

Only Shobrooke lasted until the Second World War, when a terrifying night of fire extinguished for ever the neat 18th century house. Then it joined the rest as a memory – and a level site surrounded by stately trees in which the crows everlastingly mourn.

Membland Hall, in its heyday

Membland

'Kings and Queens and an Empress have all spent holidays at Membland, and million-aires have owned it and lived there. Surely some use other than complete demolition should be its ultimate fate.'

THUS ended the agent's brochure offering Membland Hall for rent. This cry from the heart sounds alarm bells; a note of desperation creeps in. "Membland Hall is vacant" the particulars tell us. "It is ideally constructed and situated for an hotel or school. Rent can be arranged on a sliding scale." Desperate indeed, for as the same particulars pointed out – "It is TO LET for any suitable purpose at a ridiculous percentage on cost, and at even less than its intrinsic value as a lead, slate and metal mine." But despite the claims that the estate was more salubrious than Torquay, that palms grew in the grounds and that there was no other large hotel nearer than Plymouth, no tenant came forward, and no other use was found for the deserted house.

This was in the 1920's – at a time when the country was still recovering from the First World War, when the landed gentry were coming to terms with the loss of their cosy, self-indulgent life that had seemed so permanent, so safe. Circumstances were indeed reduced for many of them, and the loss of almost a complete generation of menfolk brought hardships of another kind. Labour was in very short supply and even those with money aplenty could no longer keep estates running in the old accustomed manner. Houses such as Membland, far from being the desirable residences so glowingly described, were more likely to prove an expensive millstone round the neck – and there were plenty to choose from!

Membland and the name of Baring seem forever linked in most people's memories. It is as if the estate had no existence before or after; no other owners; just the thirty-odd year span of Revelstoke domination. And yet … a house must have existed since at least the sixteenth century. Lysons records that the manor was owned by a family of the name Membland, "then it passed to the Hillersdons, then to Champernowne, who sold it in 1723. It was bought by Bulteel in 1757, and later by Perring, who rebuilt the house" and left it to his nephew Sir John Perring Bt.

An account written in 1936 by Mr G W Copeland, which appeared in *The Transactions* of the Devonshire Association, describes how the author, poking around the then ruined house, of which only the wings remained in a 'battered condition', came across "the portions of an ancient granite arch belonging to a fireplace. A little handwork revealed further portions of it and it seemed to belong to a much earlier house of between the 15th and 16th centuries." The author suggested this had been the fireplace of a principal ground floor room as the later house had been raised a storey. He records that the arch was removed and incorporated in a room in Treluggan manor house at Landrake. The only other reference to the original comes in the 1927 demolition catalogue. Lot 434, located in the kitchen passage, was "The massive granite Tudor doorway, 7ft 9in high by 5ft wide."

The correct chronology of who built or rebuilt, what, will never be known. 'Rebuilding' is a misleading term. Often it only meant revamping, putting a new facade on a venerable old house so that it appeared fashionably modern. Many a 'new' Georgian ediface, four-square, stuccoed and pillared, was simply an all-embracing jacket around a much older brick or stone-built core. Membland was almost certainly one such.

Sir John Perring, who was Lord Mayor of London in 1803 and created a baron in 1806, was recorded

Membland Hall, 1827

as living at Membland in 1811. Drawings exist of the house he created around the original Tudor manor. It had a central block with two linked wings, and bore a striking resemblance to Haldon House. The outline of that house remained beneath the Victorian veneer so lavishly applied by Edward Baring. Heavily disguised with colonnades, porticos, shutters, gabling and the dominating tower, the original house still formed the principal part.

Sir John Perring offered Membland for sale in 1827, with 1,950 acres. "The Manor of Noss Mayo, its rights, privileges and appurtenances, chief and conventionary Rents, the Game strictly Preserved. Membland House, the substantial brick-built edifice, erected on an elevation with wings, Lawns and carriage drive in front adapted for a family of Distinction." The purchaser was to take "all timber, timber-like trees, tillers and pollards down to one shilling a stick, also the coppice and underwood, and to pay for the fixtures in the mansion house, offices etc. and for all ploughing, seeding, dressing, manure and compost heaps on the lands in hand by Valuation." Buying and selling estates such as Membland must have been very complicated.

From The Times *of November 30th, 1827*

The house was reached by an "ascent of a flight of steps with double rails to a spacious entrance hall." On the ground floor were three public rooms and a WC. On the first floor were four principal bedchambers, two dressing rooms, a WC: on the upper floors were 3 bedrooms, dressing room, nursery and two servants rooms. That was all in the main block. The wings were connected by colonnades. The west wing contained the dairy, cheese room, scullery, lumber room; over which were the apple room, 3 sleeping rooms and the dairy maid's room, with the wine cellar beneath. In the east wing were the kitchen, scullery, housekeeper's room, wash-house, brewery, laundry and two bedrooms. All this was offered for sale by Mr Robins at Garraways Coffee House, Change Alley, Cornhill, in the City of London. The estimated rental of the estate was £2,400 per annum.

The details of the tenants, their holdings and annual rents, followed in great detail, for it was upon such things that the viability of large estates depended. Also mentioned in some detail were the "pleasure grounds, the capital kitchen garden, walled and clothed with choice fruit trees, standards and well stocked and cropped. A sheet of water and extensive gravelled walks, plus a melon ground and hot (with vines) and greenhouses, an outer garden and orchard."

The estate again came on the market on 31st August, 1841, with 2,020 acres and again it was auctioned in London, at The Gallery, 14 Regent Street. Apart from waxing lyrical over the salubrious climate of the South Hams, the auctioneer gives prominence to the "inexhaustible Quarry of Slate in full work, and Iron Ore recently discovered near the Coast." The Drawing Room was given as 38ft 6in by 17ft 6in with 2 statuary marble chimney pieces, flock paper hangings and gilt mouldings. The 'eating room' was 22ft by 19ft 6in with recess for sideboard, and marble fireplace.

The housekeeper's room had moved to the basement, together with the servants' hall, beer, wine, coal and cyder cellars.

One of the wings had acquired a Justice Room, and at 'at a convenient distance' were the stables, laundry and wash-house, gardener's house, two barns, cyder house and mill, drying grounds, sheds, car-

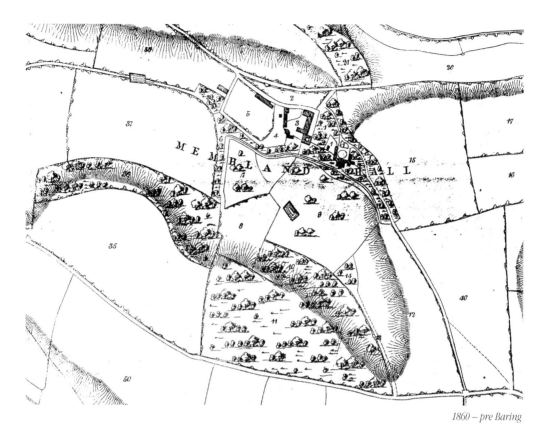

1860 – pre Baring

1895, showing new drives, new buildings, altered house and grounds

14

penter's shop, granary, cowhouse, dog kennel, piggeries etc., and the kitchen gardens. These were described as having double walls, and "most abundantly stocked with all kinds of fruit trees in high perfection." In addition there were "a range of capital hot and green-houses with vines, a fish pond, melon pit etc.; a most productive orchard and well laid out pleasure grounds ."

White's Gazette of 1878 states that Membland was formerly the seat of Robert Robertson and that in November, 1860 it was bought by John Delaware Lewis for £73,234 16s 0d.

Membland became the property of Edward Charles Baring on 26th June, 1871. At that time the house was not overlarge with only ten bedrooms and three main reception rooms, although the domestic offices seemed very numerous. By the time Baring had finished with it, Membland had 19 principal bed and dressing rooms, 18 secondary, 7 baths and 'umpteen claras', hall, drawing room, dining room, morning room, study, billiard room, smoking room and acres of servants' quarters, stables etc. (1895 Sale Catalogue). The cost of this transition must have been prodigious.

The architect chosen to revamp Membland and bring it up to the standard necessary for the lavish entertaining that was an essential part of the Baring's lifestyle, was George Devey. Baring may have been influenced by the designs Devey had prepared for Killarney House in Ireland, the property of the Earl of Kenmare, completed in 1872. Baring's daughter, Elizabeth, married Viscount Castlerosse, heir to the earldom, in 1887. The Dutch gables and some of the ornate interiors, described as "lavishly decorated with Spanish leather and wooden columns" resemble those at Membland. Killarney burnt down in 1913.

The few pictures that have survived of the interior give some idea of the sheer lavishness of the rooms. William Morris was called in to decorate Membland, and it was anticipated that this work would take two to three years to complete, "not least because of the large quantity of silk required." Unfortunately there are no records of this work or the details of the cost, but it must have been the very height of fashion! How the visiting local gentry must have stared – but it was money well spent, for those same silk hangings to the walls were still in place in 1927, and worthy of being included in the final sale. After all those years, was it possible to detach the silk from the walls? Local people recall that many a purchaser had a frustrating time trying to remove such items as the bathroom tiles, the floorings and other such fittings.

Noss Mayo, or Revelstoke, as it was sometimes called, owes much of its present day appearance to Ned Baring. Lord of the Manor he had become, and he intended it should be worthy of him. Once the house was completed he turned his attentions to the parish. He was steadily acquiring land, farms and cottages. What had been an estate of some 2,000 acres grew to around 4,500. He owned most of Noss Mayo, and 14 cottages in Newton Ferrers. All the buildings he erected are easily recognisable even though no longer painted in 'Revelstoke Blue'. Solidly constructed of stone with overhanging slate roofs, often with dormers and massive ornate chimneys, mullioned and leaded windows – even without the 'ECB' or later 'R' plaque, they are obviously part of the Membland estate. It is ironic that everything has survived, except the house itself.

There were three handsome lodges, as befitted the entrance to a great man's estate, where royalty would be a guest. The most ornate is still known as the 'Bull and Bear', built to mark the union of the Bulteel, Baring and Mildmay families. But he also lavished money on such relatively humble buildings as the laundry, the gas plant and house, the stables and kennels, and the boathouse. Thought and care went into every detail, and all are now very desirable properties.

A new church was built for the growing village, and Baring also tidied up the ruins of St Peter the Poor Fishermen, isolated on the coast, but a favourite stopping point on the 'Nine Mile Drive' con-

The billiard room, showing the organ with its painted panels

structed around the coast.

Although it was undoubtedly designed as a show place where Royalty could be entertained, it was also a much-loved family home. The Barings had ten children, born between 1862 and 1878, the first and last of whom died in infancy. What fun those youngsters must have had romping all over the estate, messing about on the estuary, visiting cousins and nearby Flete and Mothercombe. Maurice Baring, the seventh child, born in 1874, has left us a lovely, intimate picture of the house, seen through the eyes of a child.

> *Membland was a large square Jacobean house, white brick with green shutters and ivy, with some modern gables, rough cast additions and a tower. When you went through the hall you came into a large billiard room in which there was a staircase leading to a gallery going round the room. The billiard room was high and there were no rooms over it, but beyond the billiard table the room extended into a lower section culminating in a semi-circular window in which there was a large writing table. Later under the staircase there was an organ and the pipes of the organ were on the wall.*
>
> *There was a drawing room, full of chintz chairs and books, potpourri and a grand pianoforte, and next to the school room there was a little room full of rubbish which was called the Cabinet Noire where we were sent when we were naughty.*
>
> *Around Membland were several nests of relatives. Flete, Pamflete, and aunts in Yealmpton, one of whom dived under the bed when she heard carriage wheels rather than receive visitors.*

In 1878 Maurice recalls falling into the fire in his godmother's room and his little white frock caught light and his body was badly burnt – he was four at the time.

The housekeeper was called Mrs Tudgay and he describes her calm, crystal cold manner. She was thin, reserved, rather sallow and had a clear quiet precise way of saying scathing and deadly things to those she disliked. However, this did not include the children who she guarded and cared for, and he recalls baskets of food, and evenings spent playing long whist in the housekeeper's room, and sometimes wine on picnics. Both Maurice and his brother Hugo were used as models for cherubs heads carved in stone in the reredos in the new church at Noss Mayo.

He recalls that in the early days at Membland the postman walked over from Ivybridge with the post, but later it came by cart from Plympton.

"In autumn guests arrived for the cover shooting, which was good and picturesque. November was

The Schoolroom

"My Room"

The Drawing Room

"Mama's Sitting Room"

17

spent in London and then back to Membland for Christmas. The Christmas tree was first placed in the billiard room, then the drawing room, and then finally settled in the covered tennis court." The tree was lit on Christmas Eve after tea and Hugo and Maurice dispensed the presents to the servants and guests.

The family also owned a 150 ton yacht, the *Waterwitch*, in which they went to Cowes each year. It had a large dining cabin, his mother's cabin aft, a cabin for his father and three spare cabins. There was also a little steam launch called the *Wasp* used for jaunts to Plymouth. On rainy days they played hide-and-seek all over the house.

Life seemed one long round of pleasure, of parties and sporting events, of house parties and happy meetings. It must all have seemed so secure, and to a boy such as Maurice Baring his life must have seemed assured, revolving round households and families similar to his own, with endless wealth at their disposal.

The Waterwitch

But it all had to come to an end. One man's downfall affected the whole neighbourhood. For some it may have spelt ruin. Incredulous ears must have listened in disbelief as the news of the Baring collapse reached this distant corner. One wonders who was the first to hear, and how? It must have sent shock waves around the peninsula that reverberate still. There would have been no rumours, no early warning – just the bolt from the blue that rocked their world to its foundations.

In the autumn of 1890 Hugo and I went up to London for the long leave. My father and mother were at my sister's house in Grosvenor Place and there we heard about the financial crisis at Baring Brothers which had nearly ended in great disaster. When we went back to Membland for Christmas everything was different. There was no Christmas party and the household was going through a process of gradual dissolution. Cherie was leaving us, the stables were empty and the old glory of Membland had gone for ever.

It is hard for us today to envisage the influence of a clan such as the Barings. Banking had for long been considered a gentlemanly profession, and the Barings had been merchant bankers since the early 18th century. The power they wielded was enormous – governments across the globe relied on them, business enterprises prospered or failed according to their dictates; crowned heads knocked on their doors. The houses of Baring and Rothschild between them controlled most of the world's finances. Not for nothing were they likened to the ruling heads of Europe and dubbed the Sixth Great Power.

The Wasp

Their period of greatest influence and prosperity came in the 19th century when between them the various branches of the family had five peerages and two Knights of the Garter. But only Edward, or 'Ned's' branch was actively involved with the family bank, and his was the last title (Lord Revelstoke) to be conferred, in 1885.

It was said of him that he was autocratic and determined to control others. Although his was one of the smallest holdings in terms of capital, it was his hand that guided the bank's affairs, and he took one of the largest shares of the profits, indicating his degree of involvement and control. Since Rothschilds had largely taken over the European markets, Barings looked across the Atlantic to America and to the developing nations of South America. But loans were at the mercy of unstable and often, to the banking world, unethical governments who saw no reason to honour debts incurred by a previous government.

In 1873 they took a step that seemed relatively unimportant at the time, but was to have the most dire consequences. They despatched to Buenos Aires as their agent for an initial three years, Nicholas Bouwer, a clerk of Dutch extraction, who had been with Barings for some 13 years. He it was who made assessments 'on the ground', who followed the progress of the various development schemes against which Barings had lent massively and who was supposed to keep an experienced eye on wily governments. Financing such loans was not easy as the British public were more cautious than Barings and did not like to trust their money to the cauldron of South American politics, and Barings in many instances found themselves holding huge numbers of unsaleable shares.

By 1890 it was increasingly obvious to Barings that they were in trouble, although hardly anyone in the City was aware of their problems. Even when it became common knowledge that the affairs of the Argentinian and Uruguayian governments were heading for a fall, no-one believed it would take Baring Brothers with them. Worst of all, Lord Revelstoke shared this view and thought they could carry through.

But they did not. The crisis came in October, 1890, and the senior banking figures gathered – it is said that the first indication the City had of the impending crash was the appearance of such figures as Lord Rothschild in the City early on a Saturday morning. They and the Bank of England were anxious to avert complete collapse as this would destroy the credibility of London as the centre of the business world.

The rescue was effective, and Barings as a house was saved. But Lord Revelstoke had no part in the recovery of Baring Brothers, which by the end of the century was again a force to be reckoned with world wide. It is perhaps a little too harsh to blame Lord Revelstoke entirely for the crash, although his was the controlling power. Communications in those days were erratic, slow and unreliable – a great trust and responsibility must inevitably have been reposed on the man on the ground. Those in London could only hope that all was well. In an age of instant communications, of faxes, computers, telephones etc. it is hard to understand how international business was ever conducted without them – and why there weren't more such disasters as that which overtook the House of Baring.

A price had to be paid, and that price was Membland and Lord Revelstoke's pride. The estate was valued at £150,000 with a further £10,000 for the contents. The London property at 37 Charles Street, (now the English Speaking Union headquarters) was also forfeit. It would appear that these properties passed into the ownership of the Bank, and that Lord Revelstoke was allowed to occupy them. By a Deed of Pole dated 26th April, 1895, the estate passed to his eldest son, John. It was in this year that the

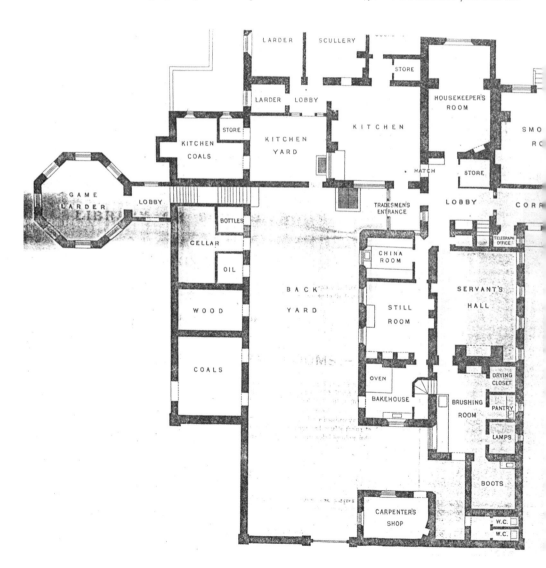

first attempt was made to sell the estate. The catalogue describes Membland as a fine old-fashioned mansion for sale in one lot, with 4,135 acres. From this, and the many subsequent sale catalogues that charted the downward progress of the house, it is possible to build up a picture of Membland in all its glory.

The inner hall (40ft x 26ft) was used as the billiard room in the Baring's time. It was largely painted white and must have been most impressive. The staircase, which rose to a galleried landing, was described as "artistic white-painted, 5ft 8in wide". The organ fitted under the quarter landing, and was enclosed by a pair of mahogany doors with interior frescoes on linen depicting 'music' and 'poetry'. A feature of considerable impact must have been the two polished Devonshire marble columns, 9ft 10in tall, with two pilasters, all in the Roman Doric design accompanied by balustrading. The fireplace, in white-painted pine, had an overmantel of two columns and two pilasters of the Ionic order –

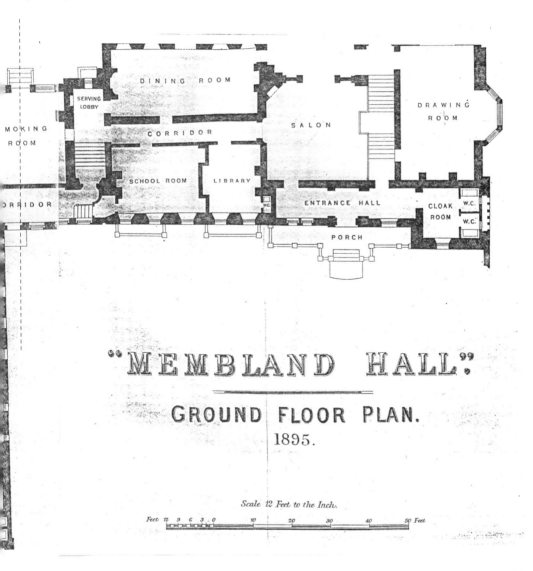

"MEMBLAND HALL."

GROUND FLOOR PLAN.

1895.

Scale 12 Feet to the Inch.

Feet 12 9 6 3 0   10   20   30   40   50 Feet

complete height 9ft 10in, and overall width 6ft 2in, with De Morgan pattern tiled surrounds and hearth and moulded marble curb.

The outer hall, by contrast, was very colourful. Part was decorated in green and gold, the whole being surrounded by a "three foot red and gilt painted dado, the walls above being covered with flock paper painted red, the floor paved with black and white marble." Both outer and inner halls were heated by hot water coils.

The Drawing room (32ft x l9ft 6in) was all white and gilt. The 1927 catalogue gives us a good idea of how it must have looked.

The ceiling paintings were of female figures with a centrepiece representing the sky.

The doors to the dining room were typical of those throughout the ground floor –

6ft 11in by 3ft 3in by 2in, three panelled, with wide

The staircase – Lord Revelstoke looking down

The ornate staircase hall

panelled linings, heavy bolection moulded architraves and CHOICELY CARVED AND DENTAL MOULDED OVERDOORS ON BOTH SIDES with antique brass furniture.' The colour scheme in the dining room (37ft by 17ft by 11ft high) was blue and gold with the dado surmounted by antique Flemish leather paper – not mentioned in the 1927 sale – with ornamental plaster ceiling, polished oak floor with another De Morgan marble and tiled fireplace. There was a carved and shaped sidetable "after the style of William Kent" with a marble top and bevelled plate glass mirror above.

The private study is described as having a panelled dado 6ft 3in high with the wall above beautifully painted by hand. There was a painted secretaire with mahogany fall-front and a painted bookcase with broken pediment top enclosed by glazed panelled doors and lined with red baize. This room also contained in a recess, a bath and w.c.

In the adjoining room, variously described as the library, morning room or school room, a Regency period fireplace survived.

The principal bedrooms were of an equally high standard. In the 1927 catalogue they are referred to as Lord Revelstoke's bedroom, the Louis XV Room with a chimneypiece after the style of Grinling Gibbons, Queen Alexandra's bedroom, hung with pink striped silk damask, and King Edward's in green with yet another white statuary marble fireplace of Italian sculpture. All the bathrooms were tiled, many with hand-painted tiles; most had marble fitments and fireplaces.

The second floor was given over to the maidservants' bedrooms, the day nursery, a box room and two batchelor bedrooms. The tower contained three further bedrooms.

From the 1926 catalogue (both pictures)

DRAWING ROOM.

284   A 7 ft. 3½ in. × 3 ft. 1 in. × 1¾ in. MAHOGANY VENEERED SIX-PANELLED DOOR, with antique brass furniture, including the panelled linings and THE RICHLY CARVED WHITE AND GILT ARCHITRAVES AND OVER-DOOR.

285   A PAIR OF MAHOGANY VENEERED THREE-PANELLED DOORS, 7 ft. 3½ in. × 4 ft. 2½ in. × 1¾ in., with antique brass furniture, including the panelled linings, THE RICHLY CARVED ARCHITRAVES AND OVER-DOORS BOTH SIDES.

286   THE WHITE AND GILT DECORATIVE PANELLING TO CEILING, AFTER THE STYLE OF ADAMS BROS., with 13 panelled paintings by Turner Lord (size of ceiling about 31 ft. × 17 ft. 6 in. (bay window in addition).

287   THE MASSIVE CARVED WHITE AND GILT WOOD CHIMNEY-PIECE, DECORATED IN THE STYLE OF ADAMS BROS., with large bevelled plate glass mirror overmantel, with 6 display shelves lined green plush and surmounted by broken pediment top. Including the two Ionic design pilasters at either corner of breast and the two lower mahogany china cupboards on either side. The chimney-piece has white marble slips (opening 4 ft. 10½ in. wide × 3 ft. 11 in. high), and including the tiled surrounds and hearth. (Total width of chimney breast 10 ft. 9 in.) (See illustration, page 17.)

288   THE WHITE AND GILT DECORATIVE PANELLING TO WALLS AFTER THE STYLE OF ADAMS BROS., including the white and gilt decorated wood dental cornice and carved skirting (size of room, 32 ft. 3 in. × 19 ft. 2 in. (bay window extra). The eight electric light brackets are included in this lot.

289   THE CARVED WHITE AND GILT SEGMENTAL SCREEN IN THE STYLE OF ADAMS BROS., 13 ft. high × 12 ft. 6 in. wide.

290   A 4-ft. SHERATON INLAID MAHOGANY CABINET, 6 ft. high, enclosed by pair of panelled and glazed doors, interior lined green plush and fitted 3 mahogany adjustable shelves.

291   A DITTO DITTO

292   Two large casement Windows (in either side of bay), each 9 ft. high × 4 ft. wide, with 2 pairs of 2-in. glazed sashes and transomes.

293   A ditto ditto (in centre of bay) together with 2 fixed side-lights.

294   A large French casement Window, with fixed side-lights and transomes, 10 ft. 6 in. high × 8 ft. wide.

295   The excellent pitch-pine Flooring as laid (principally in 3½-in. widths), about 6 squares super.

296   A dwarf four-panelled Door behind the organ, and including the moulded painted pine panelling to small lobby.

From the 1926 catalogue

     A typical feature of such houses was the segregation of the sexes – especially in the servants' quarters. At the end of the house, approached by a separate staircase, were 9 women servants' rooms with bathroom, w.c., linen room, etc. and approached by another staircase were 7 menservants rooms with bathroom and w.c.

     The Revelstoke servants seem to have been particularly well provided for, not only in the number of rooms and bathrooms but in the spacious domestic offices, which took up at least, if not more, ground space than the principal rooms of the mansion.

The domestic offices, which are quite shut off from the principal rooms, are ample and well arranged and include a large servants hall, housekeepers room with w.c., a brushing room, drying closet, lamp room, pantry, boot room, spacious kitchen, store room, scullery, meat and pastry larder, still room, bakehouse, china room.

In the basement are six cellars, a decanting room, butler's pantry, strong room, valet's sitting room, housemaids sitting room in which is the water heating apparatus for the bathrooms.

From the 1926 catalogue

Outside were the bottle house and cider cellars, the oil room, wood and coal houses, box room and game larder for 2,000 head, and the gun room.

Ice for the summer months was provided by an icemaking machine in an ice house.

Electric light throughout the house was supplied from a 12 hp gas engine and dynamo with extensive batteries. The house was also supplied with gas from a private works situated over a quarter of a mile away (for safety reasons) consisting of 5 retorts, purifier, meter house and coal house of stone and slate, and two holders.

Close by is a capital modern stone and slate cottage occupied by the gas man.

First class modern steam laundry with five room cottage, receiving and packing room, washing house, steam drying room, ironing room, boiler house, coal store, ash house and w.c., the whole being fitted with Messrs Bradford & Co most improved modern appliances and is surrounded by extensive drying ground.

The water supply to the mansion and other buildings is from a spring water stored in 2 reservoirs containing 54,000 gallons and 36,000 gallons situated at the top of the hill at the back of the house. There is also a pump fixed at the pond in front of the house from which an entirely different supply could be raised if necessary. (This was largely a fire-fighting precaution.)

Small sewage farm at sufficient distance from the house, and all sanitary arrangements are good.

The stabling comprised two distinct establishments. The household stabling included 16 stalls, 3 looseboxes, washing box, cleaning room, 2 harness rooms and large double coach house and covered washing yard with accommodation for 3 helpers, mess room, coachman's quarters with 6 rooms and extensive lofts.

Also listed were the 173ft orchard house, a range of hot pits, two vinerys of 108ft and 102ft, a fern house, numerous greenhouses including two of 194ft each arranged under one of the garden walls; a stable, cart shed, moss room, 2 closets, boiler house, mushroom house, potting and packing shed, 2 helpers bedrooms, living room and kitchen.

The hunting stable consisted of 10 looseboxes, sick box, covered washing yard, shoeing shop, 2 fodder stores, coach house, saddle room with grooms quarters over.

A picture builds up of a vast complex. Here was an estate self-sufficient in almost every detail, giving employment to a large number of local people. For much of the year Membland would have ticked over, with a nucleus of staff to keep things going. But when the family came down, everything would have come to life with a hustle and bustle as the silver was polished up, the covers taken off the best furniture, the china brought out ready for use, flowers placed around the house, and all those beds made up with the best linen sheets. It is not surprising that a house the size of Membland needed a

large laundry with 'extensive drying grounds'. The influx of aristocratic guests would have doubled the resident household – for every lord and lady would have a valet and a maid, a groom and possibly a coachman, all to be accommodated and fed.

A visit from Royalty must have caused an incredible amount of extra work, and presumably a

Two undated views of some of the servants

Queen's dresser would have taken precedence over Lady Revelstoke's maid in the Servants' Hall. Of huge importance were the game records; sporting was paramount in that late Victorian era. The 1895 catalogue gave figures for the three previous years and for the 1890-91 season: 4,360 pheasants, 55 partridge, 151 hares, 126 rabbits, 49 woodcock and 63 various were accounted for. The previous year showed 256 partridge and 630 rabbits – which figure did not include the 1,500 to 2,000 rabbits killed largely in the warren.

The pleasure grounds boasted a tennis court, gravel walks and a covered lawn tennis court at the top of the garden with an asphalt floor, provided with a dressing room, lavatory, balconies and lit by gas. From an agreement signed by Lord Revelstoke's son in 1899, we learn it had 14 bronze gas brackets and 3 gas centre lights with weights and chains, 2 bronze gas pendants and globes in the gallery and 2 heating stoves. There was also a private cricket ground with ornamental pavilion.

And at different points around the coast were cottages with spacious tea and luncheon rooms – all part of the nine mile drive created by Lord Revelstoke. The same catalogue lists most of Noss Mayo, with the exception of the church, chapel and school, plus 14 properties in Newton Ferrers.

One man's private kingdom up for sale.

Membland did not find a buyer. Lord Revelstoke had made it too magnificent, too costly for a local purchaser, and Devon has always been too remote to attract another such as he. It was only family ties that had brought the Barings there. Membland was doomed. One man had made it what it was and without him, its days were numbered.

Maurice Baring does not tell us much of those last years. How did Lady Revelstoke feel, living amongst those who had known her since childhood, her shame apparent for all to see? Did the villagers still doff their caps to them as they drove by? Was there any money left over for a few luxuries, a few good times?

By some arrangement, the family continued to live at Membland, and only two years after the crash, Lady Revelstoke died there. She was buried in the church at Noss Mayo. Lord Revelstoke joined her in July 1897. His health had been deteriorating for some years (he was diabetic) and he died at Charles Street in London. A special train brought his body home to Membland and it was said at his death that his estate was worth £35,422 17s 1d.

In May, 1899 a three day sale was held of the contents of Membland, on whose instructions is not clear. But at its conclusion there can have been very little left of the Membland that Lord Revelstoke and his wife had created. Over a thousand lots were listed, including a Coalport dinner service of 355 pieces, another of Crown Derby with the Revelstoke monogram, Wedgwood, Dresden porcelain – the list was endless. Vast numbers of candlesticks in china (Minton), brass etc. and kitchen lots ad nauseum. The dining room had six pairs of green cashmere lined Utrecht velvet curtains, and a Turkey carpet, 30ft by 16ft. In the boathouse was a 14ft canoe in the form of a crocodile, and a wherry with a 10ft beam to take horses and vehicles, and a floating stage.

Lot 1220 was 'Tommy', a bay gelding about 15 hands, quiet and reliable in harness.

Lord Revelstoke's portrait in a gilt frame was also for sale. The mahogany dining table, extending to 20ft 6in was included, but no chairs anywhere to go with it.

And so it went on, right down to the 2 doz geraniums in pots, and the gardening tools.

The exact date of the sale of Membland is not known, but it must have been around 1900. Nor is it known how much the denuded house fetched. So empty those rooms must have looked, where once Royalty and the cream of the county had been entertained. The 2nd Lord Revelstoke camped out in one corner, and the housekeeper in another. Never again was Membland to be a proper home.

"Mama"

"Papa"

MEMBLAND, SOUTH DEVON.

8 miles from Ivybridge (main line G.W.R.) and 4 from Yealmpton (branch) Railway Stations.

A CATALOGUE OF THE MAGNIFICENT

HOUSEHOLD FURNITURE

AND EFFECTS,

Including BEAUTIFUL INLAID CHIPPENDALE, ORMOLU-MOUNTED, CARVED OAK AND MAHOGANY FURNITURE; CARVED OAK CHEST; Beautifully Carved MAHOGANY ORGAN STOOL, designed by Mr. Harry Hems;

A SEMI-GRAND SEVEN-OCTAVE PIANO

(By John Broadwood & Son) in splendid Inlaid Chippendale Case;

GRAND ORGAN, by Hele & Sons, Plymouth;

THE APPOINTMENTS OF THIRTY-FIVE BEDROOMS;

Handsome Carved Mahogany Ormolu-mounted Bureaux, Bookcases and Secrétaires; Dresden, Copenhagen, Chelsea, Crown Derby, Wedgwood and other China; Oriental Jars;

PAIR OF PAINTINGS IN OILS: "THE FIVE WISE AND FIVE FOOLISH VIRGINS,"

EARLY DUTCH SCHOOL, IN SPLENDID GILT FRAMES:

EXQUISITE EMBROIDERED VELVET WINDOW CURTAINS (from the School of Art, S. Kensington);

Utrecht Velvet, Silk Damask, Tapestry and other Window and Portière Curtains; Axminster, Kidderminster, Persian, Turkey and other Carpets and Rugs;

Massive Portable STEEL FIRE GRATES, with Brass Standards and Knobs;

GREENHOUSE PLANTS, GARDEN VASES, ETC.;

STANHOPE PHAETON; Brass-mounted Double and Single Harness; Building Materials, &c.

MR. WILLIAM PEARSE

Has received Instructions from the RIGHT HON. LORD REVELSTOKE, TO SELL BY AUCTION,

On TUESDAY, MAY 30th, 1899, and following days,

ON THE PREMISES,

The Valuable Contents of the above Mansion.

On View (by Catalogue) on Tuesday, Wednesday and Thursday, the 23rd, 24th and 25th May, between 11 a.m. and 5 p.m.

SALE TO COMMENCE EACH DAY AT 11-0 A.M.

CATALOGUES, **6d.** each, may be obtained of the Auctioneer, and at Membland, on the days of viewing

☞ Intending Purchasers are requested to take particular notice of such Lots as they may wish to purchase, as the Auction of Household Furniture will be held each day in the Tennis Court, the Lots remaining where they now are, with the exception of the lighter articles.

Norwich Union Fire and Life Insurance Offices, Stoliford, Modbury, May 6th, 1899.

J. H. KEYS, PRINTER AND STATIONER, WHIMPLE ST., PLYMOUTH.

And in the end to what purpose? What was achieved by the forced sale, the disposal of the contents, the priceless furnishings, and the humiliation of the owners? The contents sale can only have realised a fraction of the true value of the items sold – the furniture, the paintings, the sculptures, the china and porcelain, all so lovingly and painstakingly accumulated over many years, the collection of a couple long married with a large family and distinguished circle of acquaintance. By 1895 Baring Brothers had been saved and was on the road to recovery – and even if it had not been, the sum realised would have been a drop in the ocean of their liabilities.

Between the crash in 1894 and 1899 a series of indentures were drawn up between the Baring Estate Co (two of the directors were Lord Revelstoke and Henry Bingham Mildmay), one of which mentions the 'old firm of Baring Brothers which was in existence prior to 1896, and the Baring Estate Company Limited, a company which was in process of voluntary liquidation.'

The last owner of the estate as such was William Cresswell Gray, a shipping magnate from West Hartlepool. A hefty legal document drawn up by the solicitors acting for William Gray lists the legal procedures whereby the Membland Estate passed from Lord Revelstoke's ownership to their client. On 15th December, 1899, an indenture was drawn up between five members of Barings, of 8 Bishopsgate, London – the Vendors – and John Headon Stanbury of Heavitree, Devon – the Purchaser – in consideration of the sum of £68,000. There had been an earlier indenture in November, 1894 between the Baring Estate Co, and two other parties, and John Stanbury, and there were several subsequent mentions of mortgages; it seems Mr Stanbury borrowed £43,000 from John Oglander and Bertram Ogle (the first mortgagees), £2,000 from the Hon Eliza Calthorpe (the second mortgagee) and a further sum from Thomas Bulteel and Mackworth Praed Parker (the third mortgagees) as these are all mentioned in the final indenture when they were to be repaid from the sale money. But were these in addition to the original £68,000 or did they form a part of it?

On 25th June, 1900, Membland became the property of William Cresswell Gray who paid £105,000 for it.

It would seem his main interest was the sporting rights and presumably the income from the land. He visited his new property only in the shooting season and preferred to stay at Point House in the village, rather than in his new mansion. The cost of furnishing Membland and making it once more habitable was probably too great for such limited use, and there are no memories of Mrs Gray or any family parties. But he played his part as Lord of the Manor. Jack Crocker, born in 1906, whose father worked on the estate, remembers their kitchen table piled high with pheasants after a day's shoot, and it was his job as a child to help his father deliver them – a brace to everyone in the village!

This genial Yorkshire squire performed another act of generosity. In a letter dated June, 1917, he informed his tenants that "In recognition of the honour His Majesty has recently been kind enough to bestow on me, I have decided to bestow a bonus of 5% of annual salaries on the business estates and to my household and estate employees, with a maximum of £5 to any one individual, signed Wm C Gray, West Hartlepool."

But it would seem the abundance of game and the presence, it was rumoured, of a lady-love at Battery Cottage, were insufficient to keep the newly created baronet's interest. He had made one attempt in 1915 to sell the Estate and 2,722 acres as a whole. It failed to find a buyer, not surprisingly with the country at war. The house was used as an officer training camp at this time. He then sealed the fate of the house by offering almost the entire estate for sale in 83 lots. Knight, Frank & Rutley's particulars list the holdings, their acreages, gross rents and outgoings, the price realised and the purchaser. Lot 1, Membland Hall with 505 acres and a gross rental value of £2,484 5s, failed to find a buyer. Many of the farms were sold to Plymouth Co-operative Society, and several of the tenants managed to buy their own holdings. The Bull and Bear Lodge was sold for £310 to Andrew Rogers; Point House made £500, The Globe Inn, £575, and the Swan Inn, £625. Rowden Farm was the most expensive at £8,100 (J Walkham the purchaser) and Coulston Farm went to the Co-operative for £6,700. In all, the sale grossed £56, 515.

In 1921, Messrs Knight, Frank & Rutley were again instructed to sell Membland Hall estate, together with 505 acres, at the Royal Hotel, Plymouth. This included Pool Mill Dairy Farm, Pool Mill Farm, and the Post Office Farm. From the photos in the particulars, the house and grounds still seem well maintained with a neat and productive kitchen garden. Lot 1, again, was Membland Hall, and again, it did not sell. Sir William therefore withdrew the Agent's house, Gas Cottage and land, the Hunting Stables and the woodland adjacent to the house. He still hoped to find a buyer for it as a small country estate and did not want to jeopardize that possibility.

But Pool Mill Farm, Pool Dairy Farm, Post Office Farm and odd enclosures brought him a further £11,185.

Three years later came the final sale. On 23rd October, 1924, at 2.30pm precisely, Knight, Frank & Rutley again offered Membland Hall for sale at the Royal Hotel in Plymouth. There were no reserves, and although the same photographs were used, the size of the particulars and their presentation had shrunk, the Hall itself being disposed of in just three small pages. Lots 1, 2 and 3, comprising the house, outbuildings, agent's house and kitchen gardens, and the hunting stables, were sold for £2,800 to George Coyle, or Coyte. Gas Cottage made £1,100, and the same purchaser, S H Wright, paid a similar

1584

Membland Hall ESTATE.

Sir Wm Cresswell Gray Bart: Devonshire

LOT.	DESCRIPTION.	AREA.			GROSS RENT.			OUTGOINGS.			NET RENT.			RESERVE.			PURCHASE PRICE.		
		A.	R.	P.	£	s.	D.	£	s.	D.	£	s.	D.	£	s.	D.	£	s.	D.
	Mansion, Gardens ch.																		
1-3	Lots 1, 2 & 3.	63	2	18				17	7	0							2800		
4	Western Lodge & Land	29	0	4				4	11	5							1100		
5	Accommn & Wood land	29	1	9				3	18	5							700		
6	Gas Cottage & Land	17	2	8				2	7	5							1100		
7	Laundry Cottage & land	5	2	33					13	4							625		
8	Pasture field opposite.	6	1	15				1	4	9							425		
9	Pasture field adjoining	8	0	15				1	11	2							450		
10	Arable Field	18	0	2				3	8	4							230		
11	Accommodation land	21	2	28				4	3	3							560		
12	Part of "The Grove"	16	0	20					12	7							260		
13	Part of Membland Wood	11	3	37					10	3							260		
		227	2	0				40	17	11							8510		

From Knight Frank & Rutley's 1924 sale records

amount for Western Lodge. Laundry Cottage went for £625, and in, total another £8,510 went into Sir William Gray's account.

And thus ended his association with Membland which he had bought as a fine gentleman's sporting estate, and left as a desolate shell.

The final chapter in the history of Membland is all too familiar. Without its estate to support it, a house of such proportions was not economic. According to local information, the house was bought by Stanley Pitts, who paid £2,000 for the Hall and its outbuildings. He was the brother of William Pitts, the maltster who had kept the estate supplied from his brewery down on the quay. One final brochure offered Membland for rent. There is no date, and no agent's name. The fourteen pages seem more of a tribute to Lord Revelstoke, and one last desperate plea for his home.

> *At great outlay he consolidated the property, paying in some cases sixty years' purchase of the annual value. At greater expense he improved it and more substantial and picturesque buildings than those he erected for his tenantry it is impossible to find. Church, Post Office, School, Roads, Bridges, Lodges, show art combined with means have provided an everlasting memorial in this lovely country of this open-handed, big-hearted man.*

An interesting comment is made on the marine drive. "This drive was constructed during hard times as a sort of relief works, where anyone could get a job-of-work. The present day remark is 'That was a good old house, any man could get work and pay, and could take home to his family on Saturday a pheasant or a chicken as well'."

But the photographs showed the true state of affairs; the house had been empty for almost thirty years, and all trace of splendour had gone. The inside looks reasonable, but outside the ivy that Maurice

---

yal Hotel Plymouth SALE.   DATE _23ʳᵈ October 1924._

Solicitors: Messrs Turnbull & Tilley. West Hartlepool.

TOTAL PURCHASE PRICE.	DEPOSIT.	NAME OF PURCHASER.	PRIVATE TREATY INSTRUCTIONS.				
			QUOTING PRICE.	VENDOR'S INSTRUCTIONS.	SOLD AT.	DEPOSIT.	LOT.
£ s. D.	£ s. D.		£ s. D.	£ s. D.	£ s. D.	£ s. D.	
		George Coyle.					
		S. H. Wright.					
		S. H. Wright.					
		S. H. Wright.					
		H. Worth.					
		H. Worth.					
		S. H. Wright.					
		W. Salter.					
		J. P. Moore.					
		J. P. Moore.					
		S. H. Wright.					

Membland in 1927

Baring remembered had got out of hand; the brambles were encroaching, and it looked a sorry picture. So, despite the offer to rent it to almost anyone for almost any sum, the story dragged on to its inevitable conclusion. The final sale catalogue was 'to dispose of the Fixtures, Fittings, Materials and Fabric of the Mansion, which will be sold in Lots for Demolition.' This was held over two days, 21st and 22nd September, 1927. Viewing was to be on the four previous days and as well as the two-manual 23 stop hydraulic organ which had remained in situ all this time, there were many thousands of Welsh and Delabole slates, 430 yards of granite paving setts, rainwater guttering and stackpipes, electrical wiring and fittings, the dynamo and engine, a 26 hp Hornsby Ackroyd oil engine, and a Geipel and Lange switchboard.

The catalogue was wonderfully detailed; the measurements meticulously given, and even the variations noted; doors were $1^{1/2}$ inches thick or $1^{1/4}$ inch, or $1^{3/8}$ inch. The contents of each room were listed, the doors, the windows, the panelling and fittings. Reading down through the endless lots, 699 in all, the sumptuousness of the rooms still leaps from the stark lists. It must have been fabulous when the Barings were still all powerful and the house newly completed.

As it looked in 1927

LOT

686 THE FABRIC OF THE MANSION, including the ground and upper floor joists, all beams and girders, stone cills and heads, chimneys and everything else which has not been previously lotted or reserved. The whole of the walls with the exception of the basement walls are built of brick; the basement walls are of granite. This Lot extends from the Drawing-room on the west side to the Larder on the east side, and down as far as the Carpenter's Shop and W.C.'s on the north side.

687 THE BRICK AND STONE ASHLAR IN THE FABRIC OF THE GUN ROOM, GAME LARDER AND COAL CELLARS on the east side of the large Courtyard, with the wall round to and including the piers to the Courtyard entrance; and includes all the SALT GLAZED AND WHITE GLAZED BRICKS in the Game Larder and Staircase leading thereto.

Conditions of Sale.

The conditions
of sale show
some of the
problems
connected with
a demolition
sale on this
scale

1. The highest bidder to be the Purchaser, and if any dispute arise between two or more bidders, the lot shall, at the discretion of the Auctioneer, be put up again at the last undisputed bidding and re-sold, the Auctioneer's decision on all matters to be final. No person to advance less at each bid than the amount named by the Auctioneer, no bidding to be retracted, and the Auctioneer may refuse any bid. The vendor reserves the right to bid by himself or his Agent.

2. The Purchasers to give in their names and places of abode on the slips provided in the Catalogue and, if required, to pay down a deposit of 5s. in the £ in part payment of the purchase money, such deposit to be applicable to all or any of the lots purchased and **to pay the remainder of the purchase money not later than the 23rd day of September, 1927,** and no lot shall be removed or taken down until full payment has been made.

3. The lots are sold with all faults, imperfections, and errors of description, weight and sizes the Auctioneers not being responsible for the correct description, genuineness, or authenticity of, or any fault or defect in any lot, and giving no warrant whatever. The weights, quantities and sizes as stated are approximate only and are given merely as a guide to intending Purchasers; they are not guaranteed, and any difference arising between the actual measurements, weights or quantities and those stated shall not annul or affect the Sale.

4. The lots immediately on being sold are held as delivered to the Purchaser and remain at his, her or their risk. Transfer of Purchasers' names in the Sale Book cannot be recognised.

5. The Auctioneers reserve the right to alter the mode of lotting, to amalgamate two or more lots, to alter the order of selling from that arranged in the Catalogue and to withdraw any lot or lots from the Sale.

6. All matters of dispute, other than the immediately after-mentioned, shall be submitted to the Auctioneers, whose decision thereon shall be final and binding on all parties. All matters, disputes or claims concerning damage sustained by any Purchaser to his, her or their property, from the time of purchase, during and until removal of same, shall be settled between the Purchasers themselves, none of whom shall have any claim against the Seller on any ground whatever, and in the event of no such settlement being arrived at, such matters, disputes or claims shall be referred to Messrs. Fox & Sons, Auctioneers, Bournemouth, for whose expenses in any such reference the Purchasers concerned shall be liable and whose decision on such matters, disputes or claims, including expenses, shall be final and binding on the parties to the reference. Principals will be held responsible for the acts of their servants, employees, workmen and others.

7. Should any damage be occasioned by any Purchaser to any property of the Seller, which is either reserved or unsold, he, she or they shall make good the same or pay a sum in damages as shall be assessed by the Auctioneers.

10. No lot can be removed during the Sale or without an order from the Auctioneers.

11. On failure of complying with the above conditions, the deposit money shall be forfeited. Any lots not cleared by the time allowed may be re-sold by public or private sale, and the deficiency (if any), together with all expenses attending such re-sale, shall be made good by the defaulter at this present Sale, and shall be recoverable as liquidated damages.

Note.—All lead, lead and iron piping, baths, cisterns, water closets and radiators are excluded from the Sale and will be removed by the owner.

From a newspaper cutting it would seem that the fabric of the mansion was not sold as such, for in 1928 it was 'pulled down in such a way as suggests gunpowder was used.' A guidebook described it thus:

Membland Hall, a commodious but never beautiful house, was pulled down for the sake of the lead in the roof, the fireplaces, staircases etc. and just the shell of it now remains, though quite a colony inhabits the various lodges, the converted laundry, and stables and garden houses which grew up around the great house.

No doubt the shell was robbed of anything that could be used in the conversion of the stables and other properties. The site, and what was left of the Hall, were bought by Albert Bradford, and in 1967 he dealt the coup-de-grace and pushed the remains over into the cellars. By this time it must have been highly dangerous and an eyesore. Using some of the salvaged stone, Bert Bradford embarked on a building programme. Game House incorporated part of the original wall of the mansion, the covered tennis court became flats, and Manor Court went up on the tennis court site, and is still lived in by Bert's daughter and her husband, Mr & Mrs Paine.

If Lord Revelstoke could return, he would recognise much of his handiwork around the parish; his nine-mile drive is part of the coastal footpath, the lodges and gates with his monogram are all intact and there are reminders of the Baring era everywhere.

The Gardeners' Chronicle of February, 1885, gives an interesting account of the newly planted grounds of Lord Revelstoke's estate.

A lodge, recently erected, substantial, elaborate and original in design, indicates the entrance to the park. The circuitous drive with a gradual descent leading from the sea coast brings one to the house. Benefitting by the experience of the adjoining estate proprietors, Pinus insignis has been extensively planted and on the right side of the drive mentioned, it has been planted at a distance of 40ft apart the whole length. Picea Normanniana and other pinuses are planted between, these

Lady Revelstoke and her youngest daughter Susan as a bride

to be eventually cut as the Pinus insignis increases in growth. Membland maybe said to be only in its infancy judging from the preparations for planting, the cutting and laying out of new drives etc. and although much work has been accomplished within the last few years, it has only of late years passed into the hands of the present proprietor who seems to be quite alive to the manner by which the natural surroundings may be made still more interesting and enjoyable by judicious planting.

The article then describes the '8 mile drive', commencing from the lodge referred to and describes its progress along the coast and views obtained from it.

Large additions have been made by the present owner to the old building, the improvements and additions being in the same style of architecture as the old portion. Although the house is situated so near the sea, yet no glimpse of it can be seen from it. A thick belt of oak blocks out the view and protects the house from the gales.

The pleasure grounds fronting the house are not extensive neither are they required to be, the natural surroundings are themselves of sufficient attraction for those who love and enjoy rural scenery. The lawn in front is one bold slope of grass only bounded by a link fence. Trees and shrubs are neatly dis-

The terrace in the Baring's time

pensed with in this instance and wisely so, the bold scenery of hills and valley near and far requiring no aid from dressed grounds of small Coniferae to enhance its grandeur. The walls, pillars and porticos are covered with ivy intermingled with Ampelopsis Veitchii, Lonicera Veitchii, Lonicera Frangrantissima and other climbers and below both the terrace walls large plants of Fuchsia Riccartonii were flowering splendidly.

The writer describes in detail the glass houses – 18 in total for vines, peaches, cut flowers, pot plants, exotics, propagating and no 13 filled with double white primulas, no 14 with double pelargoniums and no 16 entirely given over to tomatoes.

Lord Revelstoke

Source material

The archives of Baring Brothers, now Ing Barings, London; Sir Alexander Reid Bt., RHS Lindley Library; Westcountry Studies and West Devon Record Office; Devon & Exeter Institution; sale catalogues from private sources; 'The Sixth Great Power', Philip Zeigler

A newly completed Lindridge

Lindridge

THE fire that destroyed Lindridge on 25th April, 1963, bereft the Westcountry of one of its finest architectural gems. For at least 300 years a house of significance had stood on this attractive site. Although it had been altered many times, enlarged, reduced, refaced, reroofed and its grounds developed from a natural Devon landscape to a highly complex formal garden complete with temple, lily pond, topiary and statuary, and canal-style swimming pool, yet Lindridge was always in harmony with its setting.

When the first house was built is not recorded, but the ownership of the manor stretches back to 1044 when it formed part of the holdings of the Bishops of Exeter, with whom it remained until 1549, after the Dissolution.

The approach to Lindridge from Sandy Gate is, for a mile and a half, through a beautiful hanging wood. The ancient house of Lindridge was a very large pile of building; which is said to have covered an acre of ground. (There are plain vestiges of the old building to the extent of more than half an acre.) Of this mansion the two wings and other buildings have now been pulled down, the central part only remains. But this centre is a noble house; it has two elegant fronts, and the rooms within it are large and commodious. The room which was fitted up in 1673 (as appears from a tablet over the chimney) and kept for the purpose of a ballroom, is still preserved, a monument of former festivity, though the splendour of its decorations is somewhat faded by time. It

An early view, undated

measures in the clear 50 feet by 30 feet; and its height is well-proportioned to its length and breadth. It has six windows; and its rich carved work, copper ceiling, and panels of burnished gold, are highly ornamental. The gilding alone (as appears from the old stewards book) was performed by agreement with the artist for the sum of £500.

The grounds at Lindridge are picturesque and even to the observer of taste who has wandered amidst the scenery of Ugbrook must afford new sources of pleasure, particularly the inequalities and light verdure of the lawn over which the eye though carried to a great extent, is yet relieved by flowing foliage interposed in elegant variety, the woods clothing the hills or waving in dark masses of shade from the chasms of the lime rock and the gay diversities of green exhibited in rich distinctions by the oak, the beech, the elm, the fir, the lime, the chestnut, the plane and the walnut all flourishing with uncommon vigour and seem unrivalled in Devonshire for the beauty of their growth.

John Templar was the owner in 1793 when the historian Polwhele wrote this account of Lindridge.

Richard Martin would seem to be the first owner to make Lindridge his residence and historians have attributed the building of the 'great pile' to him, although he only owned Lindridge for four years. His brother succeeded and probably completed the house. It must have been enormous, and a good deal of imagination is needed to picture two large wings on either side; as Lindridge is built into rising ground, these must have stretched towards the gardens, flanking the south front. They may even have been two separate pavilion style wings, as were built at Haldon and the original Membland. Nor do we know when they were demolished. But we do know that it was Sir Peter Lear, owner of Lindridge from 1660 to 1683, who gave to Lindridge its beautiful interiors, and created the amazing ballroom.

Originating from nearby Ipplepen, Sir Peter made himself a fortune from sugar plantations in Barbados. He did not return to England until after the Restoration whereupon he was made a baronet. Had his sugar riches helped to support the absent monarch in his exile – and were Sir Peter and his riches instrumental in the Merry Monarch's return? Certainly there seemed no shortage of money as far as Sir Peter was concerned. William Martin, the last Martin owner of Lindridge, had six daughters and it is possible that Sir Peter married one of them. If so, he set about rebuilding the family home with a vengeance.

It was a period when many large and elegant houses were built by those who had supported the Stuart cause and worked for the Restoration, and presumably claimed their reward. It is a sad fact that very few of them have survived in the Westcountry.

From the photographs of Lindridge it would seem Sir Peter must have radically altered, if not completely rebuilt, the Elizabethan house. It is so very typical of that period. The interiors were particularly fine, and Christopher Hussey, writing in *Country Life*, assumes that London craftsmen would have been called in to execute the wainscotting, the fireplaces, the exceptionally fine doorcases, and the ornamental ceilings. These deserve a special comment, for there are now very few in existence. The copper mentioned in Polwhele's description referred to the wiring which attached the plaster foliage and flora

Sir Peter Lear's Ballroom (Country Life)

to the plaster-base ceiling, giving the whole thing a suspended effect. There was a fine example at Dunsland House near Holsworthy, constructed around the same time, but it, too, was destroyed by fire.

The ballroom was an incredible room to find in this remote area of Devon, but if Sir Peter's wife was a Martin, then Lord Clifford of Ugbrooke would have been his brother-in-law, a staunch supporter of Charles II who became the Lord Treasurer. Lindridge would have to be sufficiently splendid to entertain his important relations. That beautiful room must have seen many festive occasions, many splendid gatherings when the cream of the county gathered together in their finery – to see and to be seen – though it must have been a tedious long way home when all was over.

The property remained in the Lear family until the death of the last baronet, Sir John, in 1736. It was acquired by the Rev Dr Finney, who sold it for £8,000 to John Baring of Exeter. In the late 18th century it passed via the Line family to the Templers. They were a prominent family in the Teignbridge area with quarries at Haytor on Dartmoor and interests in the port and docks at Teignmouth. Their great house was at Stover, built in 1780. Another branch acquired Lindridge in about 1790 and lived there quietly for well over a century. They appear to have left Lindridge as they found it, and it was its next owner, Lord Cable, who brought the house up to date and gave it a completely new look. Fortunately, he, too had the good taste to leave well alone so that the matchless Carolinian interiors survived.

By 1910 the Templers were no longer living at Lindridge and it had been let to William Webb for £350 per annum. The subsequent year a lease was drawn up between Captain John George Edmund Templer, who had been born at Lindridge in 1855, and Ernest Cable, at an annual rent of £380. Sir Ernest must have found the estate to his liking for in 1915 a 40 year lease was drawn up between him and John G E Templer (of Maidenhead) at the much increased rental of £643 per annum. This gave him sufficient security to immediately embark on his improvements and alterations.

Ernest Cable appears not to have had any previous connections with Devon. He had made his fortune in India, where he was born in 1859. His family were part of the merchants Bird & Co, who dealt

Prior to 1916 before refacing

in jute, coal and paper. A prosperous nabob, Cable came to England with his son and three daughters to found his dynasty.

It was not until 1920 that Lord Cable (as he had by then become) purchased the property for £75,000. This was after the First World War and after the loss of his only son, Lt Pickersgill Cable, in 1915. (The house was used by the Red Cross during the war as an officers' hospital.)

Two good photographic records remain to us, to highlight what has been lost; one is the *Country Life* article of 1938, and the other was a small brochure produced by the last owners in preparation for their grand opening to the public in Easter, 1963 – admission Adults 3/6d, Children 2/-.

Never can Lindridge have looked more lovely than when the *Country Life* photographer visited it. The trees around the house had reached maturity. Many of these were elms, and others have now fallen victim to old age and the gales. The house was immaculate and the gardens seemed at a state of perfection – if only it could have been enclosed in a capsule for all time!

If anything, the house looks almost too well cared-for, and nothing like its great age, more like an Edwardian country house. Just over twenty years earlier the external appearance of Lindridge had been radically altered. The plain stucco was removed and the entire house refaced in brick. The plain sash windows were given glazing bars and shutters, and the entrance porch enlarged. The roof parapet was removed and a round-headed window placed in the centre of the two main fronts, breaking the line of the cornice, with large stone urns placed at the corners. All the second storey windows on the south front were false. Behind them was the ballroom which occupied the whole of this front, and was double-storied in height. This work was completed by 1916.

By the outbreak of World War I, the gardens had been laid out. These were the wonder of Lindridge, and all that survives. Edward White of Milner & White, London architects, was responsible for the design of the Italian gardens that replaced the lawns in front of the house. These were extremely elaborate with

The newly laid out Italian garden

clipped yews, balustrading, wrought iron gates, complicated bedding schemes, statuary and, at the far end, a temple in the middle of a lilypond.

The sloping ground to the entrance front was also landscaped and a gravelled forecourt surrounded by hedging now gave access to the enlarged portico. The slope was terraced, and a swimming pool in the form of a canal with a temple pavilion at the far end provided a striking feature. It was shaded by towering cedars, of which there were many around the grounds. Higher still was a covered rose walk, flower gardens and the tennis court.

After the War the Cables returned to Lindridge and in 1920 Ruth Cable married Edward Benthall. The Benthalls were an ancient family from Benthall Hall, near Broseley in Shropshire (now owned by the National Trust).

Sir Edward and Lady Benthall took on the family business in India, which survived until that country's independence when it was nationalised and the family left with very little. Ruth appears not have cared much for Lindridge – or for poor Edward. After leaving India, she preferred to live in the south of France, whilst it was her husband who came home to Devon. His nephew, Richard Benthall, remembers visits to the old house as a boy when it was run very much as a batchelor establishment. The money had run out and there were few servants and fewer luxuries.

Richard also recalls that on Ruth's infrequent visits, she occupied the attic floor. Most of the principal rooms were shut up and they seem to have lived a hand-to-mouth existence. But Richard does remember jolly holidays spent at Lindridge, enjoying the sporting facilities, for which it was well known, and of impromptu dances in the ballroom, which was also used for meetings although it had very little furniture in it by this time.

Sir Edward died in 1961, and their son, Michael, became the next owner. He inherited his mother's

The altered entrance front

dislike of Lindridge. An artistic man, he was a director of the Old Vic Theatre in London and his life revolved around the stage. He had no use for a large expensive house so far from London and only visited occasionally, bringing down parties of theatrical friends, including Robert Helpman, with whom he eventually departed to Australia. Inevitably he decided to sell and in December 1961 Lindridge was put on the market. On 4th May, John D Wood auctioned 1,208 acres with sporting rights over 1,765 acres, 'at present producing £1,462 per annum but capable of substantial improvement.' The house, gardens and two farms (sold to sitting tenants) were sold for £60,000 to the Corthorn Land and Timber Co – the inevitable timber merchants. Immediately they resold the house and 60 acres to Mr John Brady of Brixham for £15,750.

Despite its vicissitudes, being used as a hospital in the First World War and as a school in the Second, Lindridge still contained many of its priceless fittings and furniture. Following the sale of the house, Lady Benthall removed the best and most portable items to Sotheby's. These included an Agra carpet specially woven for the Delhi Durbar in 1911 and brought home by Lord Cable; Georgian and Chippendale furniture, mirrors, chairs – all of which had probably been in the house for centuries. Certainly the great grandfather clock had stood in the hall since the

The wedding of Ruth Cable to Edward Benthall, 1920. Lord Cable is seated to the right of Ruth, with the bridegroom standing between them.

day it was installed in the 1780's. At least it was saved from destruction and maybe ticks away somewhere still. In June the remaining contents were sold off in a three day sale that was reported in *The Western Morning News* of 29th June, 1962.

> There were 130 lots of linen and blankets; the grand Bluthner piano (£250), an inlaid mahogany extending dining table, a revolving 2-tier dumb waiter on a stand, and six antique mahogany hall chairs. An oriental dinner service made £87 10s, a pair of Chinese vases £60, and in total over £5,000 was realised. A magnificent glassdrop chandelier was sold, and there were over 3,000 volumes of books. Outdoor effects included 250 pots of arum lilies, orchids and geraniums, and 3,000 plant pots.

Another report stated that the sale realised £17,908, and that the chandelier fetched £4,200 – it was 5ft 6in high and 3ft 9in wide and must have hung in the ballroom.

Whilst this was going on, the Corthorn Land & Timber Co were busy felling. Some of the tenant farmers were given notice to quit as the company had plans to develop the land.

Mr Brady, the new owner of Lindridge, was greeted with some relief when it was learned that he planned to restore the mansion to its former glory. *The Western Morning News* reported that he had

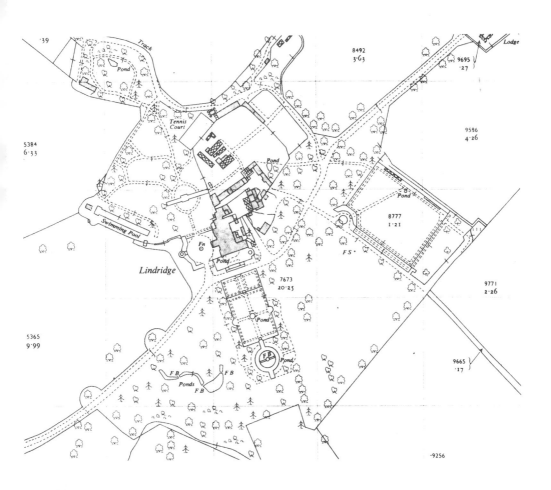

43

The ballroom prior to 1916

The same room utilised as a convalescent ward, c1916

…and refitted as a billiard room later

called upon the skills of Professor H O Corfiato from London University, an expert in classical architecture, to advise him, and he was planning to live there with his wife and daughter when it was completed. Mr Brady was reported as saying that to defray some of the considerable expense Lindridge would be opened to the public. 'I feel a place like this is part of our national heritage and that as many people as possible should be able to enjoy it,' he is reported as saying. They were less pleased when it was learnt that he was planning to erect a hundred luxury chalets in the grounds and when he finally put in an application there were 250 objections.

The grounds must have been opened to the public in that last summer of 1962, for the colour cover of Mr Brady's brochure show the swimming pool surrounded by bathers under gaily coloured parasols. The brochure was produced in time for the opening at Easter, 1963, when it was planned to open the historic house and gardens daily from 1st May. But by then it was a blackened ruin.

The noise of the fire awoke the tenant, Mrs Garner, who had a flat over the garage. She ran to the nearby farm to raise the alarm, and by four a.m. there were fire engines from five stations on the scene, attempting to bring the fire under control. But

The morning after the fire (from Wilson Archive, Teignmouth, by permission of G Robbins)

it was too late. They were severely hampered by the lack of water, for the swimming pool, which was to be kept full according to the fire insurance policy, had been emptied so that it could be cleaned prior to the opening. There was no other adequate source of water and the firemen had to make do with the lilyponds!

Two years later, in December, 1965, *The Western Morning News* asked 'Does anyone want a burnt-out mansion and 47 acres of parkland with outline planning permission for a motor museum and flats? For sale at £25,000.'

Someone did – a Mr A E Harding – and in 1971 there was a planning application for a holiday and country club at Lindridge. Nothing came of this either, and for the next twenty years owners came and went and the estate slumbered. Eventually the remains were demolished and plans for luxury houses and flats on the site were approved. After a few false starts and change of developer, several large blocks now occupy the site of the ancient house, divided into appartments.

The gardens have been restored, though never again will they look as they did on that day when the *Country Life* photographer so beautifully captured them on film.

Country Life *photo of the hall*

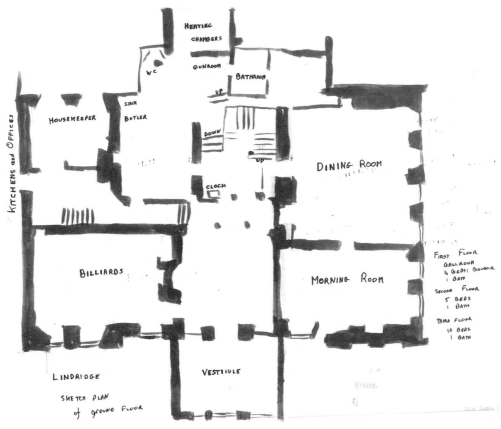

A sketch of the ground floor of Lindridge

Haldon

COUNTRY folk in Devon have a saying; 'Rags to riches and back again, in three generations.' So often it proves to be true. One hard working man to build up the family fortunes; his son to enjoy them and start spending, and the next generation to run through the lot, with no idea how to restore the vanishing wealth. The Palk family was one such.

Although they were by no means poor, the fortune amassed by Robert Palk in his years in India was quite beyond anything the family had experienced before.

Robert Palk came of yeoman stock established at Ashburton, at Lower Headborough. Here Robert was born in 1717. He was educated at Ashburton grammar school and graduated from Wadham College, Oxford in 1739. He was then ordained and as a naval chaplain accompanied Admiral Boscawen's expedition (1747) to the East Indies. The fleet remained for some time off the coast of India during which time the chaplain of Fort St David was suspended. Palk was invited to enter the Company's service as chaplain, and after obtaining the Admiralty's consent this 'very worthy and able Divine' assumed his new duties on 1st April, 1749.

Following the arrival of replacement clerics, Palk almost found himself without a job, but the Madras government, scenting a worthy administrator, quickly found him a job as Paymaster and Commissary in the Field 'at the rate of 10s a day salary and Rs 5 a day batta.' In 1755 Palk was employed as a negotiator between Colonel Lawrence and the Company. A letter dated October, 1755 sent to the Company describing Palk's activities ends thus; 'He received from Col Lawrence most beneficial employs in the camp, and by his means in other services which have, in the time of my voyage, set him independent in the world with at least £10,000 from two he came with into India. And from a month after his arrival in camp, Mr Saunders (of the Madras Government) received no further tokens of his attention or respect. Colonel Lawrence became all in all with Mr Palk'. (From MS in the possession of Mrs Bannatyne, D&E Institution)

So well did Palk conduct himself that by 1760 the directors of the Company had settled he should become the Governor when next it became vacant. In the meantime, Palk found time to return home, having been granted a coat of arms in 1760, to marry Anne, daughter of Arthur Vansittart of Shottesbrook Park, Berkshire. She was the sister of Palk's friend and former colleague, then Governor of Bengal. Lawrence, now Major General, had accompanied, and returned with him to India in 1761, and in 1763 Palk duly became Governor of Madras. His time in this office was mainly peaceful and in 1767 Palk resigned, and sailed for England with his wife and their two children, Anne, born 1764, and Lawrence, borne 1766.

It would seem that Robert Palk arrived back in Devon a wealthy man. It was the custom of the day to receive 'payments' from those hoping to receive government contracts, and rewards from those whose cause had been served – and it was rich pickings for all who knew how to keep the balance on the Indian subcontinent. Back home, he entered Parliament as member for Ashburton.

In 1769 he purchased the Haldon estate. The house had been built by Sir George Chudleigh about 1720 and after his death in 1738 the property passed in succession to Sir John Chichester, Mrs Basset, Mr John Jones and Mr William Webber. A friend congratulated him on the cheapness of his purchase, telling him that Webber had given Jones £11,500 for Haldon. Palk made many improvements; laid down floors of Indian redwood, planted trees in the park, and gradually acquired adjacent land. In 1786, Lawrence writing home to his

This portrait came up for auction in 1978 and was supposedly of Sur Robert Palk, by Tilly Kettle. A subsequent note states that it is possibly of his nephew, also Robert Palk

father said 'I suppose Haldon will be so entirely altered when I return it will be almost impossible for me to recognise it. I hear the winter has been remarkably severe and I hope your plantations have not been damaged.'

When not following the pursuits of a country gentleman, Palk resided in London where he had a house in Park Place, St James's. He re-entered Parliament for Ashburton in 1774, which seat he held until 1787. His friend, Stringer Lawrence, was a frequent, if not permanent guest at Haldon until his death (in London) in 1775. He was buried in the church at Dunchideock. (Mrs Bannatyne's MS)

On 19th June, 1782 Robert Palk was created baronet. His son, after leaving Oxford, travelled on the continent, and his daughter married Sir Bourchier Wrey of Tawstock, near Barnstaple. His wife, Anne, died at the age of only 50 in 1788, and Sir Robert in 1798, aged 81.

He was succeeded by his son, Lawrence, named in honour of his father's great friend General Stringer Lawrence, as were all the eldest sons until the line died out. It is said that Stringer left his fortune to this son and specified that Palk's sons should bear his name. The fortune is not authenticated, but the perpetuation of the name is, so that it is necessary to distinguish between the different generations by using either their second names as well, or giving them a number. Lawrence Palk followed his father into Parliament, sitting for Ashburton, and as well as the Haldon Estate, he also inherited the manor of Tormohon (Torquay), which Sir Robert had purchased back in 1767, before buying Haldon. It was this which was to prove the family's undoing. Lawrence began a long and expensive involvement in the development of Torquay, which was to be continued by his son and grandson.

Sir Robert Palk 1717 - 1798

Born Ashburton, S Devon. Governor of Madras. Retired to Torquay and HALDON HOUSE, nr Exeter, Devon.

Sir Lawrence Palk b 1766 - 1813

MP for Ashburton 1787 - 1812

Sir Lawrence Vaughan Palk 1793 - 1846

Sir Lawrence Palk- first Lord Haldon 1818 - 1883 (created baron 1880)

Lord Lawrence Hesketh Haldon 1846 - 1903

Sold off family estates at Haldon and Torquay. Died in London

Lord Lawrence William Haldon 1869 - 1933

Declared bankrupt - with assets "nil".

Lord Lawrence Edward Broomfield Haldon 1896 - 1938.

Died in London after undistinguished career.

The family tree

It was said that Sir Robert had concentrated on bringing his son up to be a gentleman and neglected to pass on any of his own sound business acumen. The early years of the 19th century were a time of great expansion – grandiose schemes and large ideas. The Empire was establishing and fortunes were being made – and spent.

The new baronet appears to have gone in at the deep end. Perhaps he was keen to establish the family amongst the older aristocracy of the county. For whatever reason, Torquay was to bear the stamp of Palk. The most ambitious scheme was for a new harbour and pier, built between 1803 and 1805 at an ever spiralling cost, which was to establish Torquay firmly on the map both as a naval base and as a seaside resort. No doubt large profits were anticipated from the sale of development land in the future. Maybe – but by the time he died in 1813, only 15 years after his father, the slide had begun.

Documents survive that show the sum of £30,000 had been raised 'upon trust by mortgage or other dispostions (except sale or exchange)' and in May, 1814, the new baronet and his mother, the Rt Hon Dame Dorothy Elizabeth Palk, Trustees of the will of Sir Lawrence, carried out a 'survey of auction' and a sale of assets was held on 27th and 31st May, 1814.

Lawrence Vaughan, (the 3rd baronet), continued to spend blithely. Streets and squares were named after the family, and plans were drawn up to extend the harbour. In 1832 that final ingredient for a Victorian seaside resort was proposed – a railway. By 1841 things were desperate and a mortgage settlement was created (to supplement a previous mortgage arranged in 1825), with the estate handed over to a Trust, which paid out fixed annuities to the children and dependants. Sir Lawrence fled the country, to France. His son, Lawrence, (4th baronet) became increasingly concerned, although he may not have known the true state of affairs:

> *...follies of Sir Lawrence Vaughan Palk and the indignation of his heir increased and by Autumn 1858 things were so desperate that the heir was taking legal steps to have his father declared lunatic. This measure was averted by the Trustees agreeing to turn over the Trust to trustees more acceptable to the heir ... one of the trustees decided it was his duty to stand by Sir Lawrence Vaughan and arrangements were made for him to return to England and live quietly with one of his daughters until his death in 1860. (History of Torquay, Percy Russell 1960)*

A cartoon by 'Spy' of Lawrence Palk, 1st Baron Haldon

However, despite his father's financial straits, when Lawrence succeeded, he carried on in his father's footsteps. Either he had a fresh influx of money, or he was sublimely optimistic. A yacht was built for him, and a large, new house on the heights above Torquay – and he flung himself with enthusiasm into the new railway scheme, becoming chairman of the Teign Valley Railway – a position that could hardly be denied him as he had put up £30,000 of capital. He sat as MP for South Devon from 1854 to 1868, and in 1880 he was created the first Baron Haldon. His ill-judged generosity is described in his obituary notice:

> *As lord of the manor of Tormohan, his lordship fulfilled the obligations of his high station with jus-tice and liberality. One of his first public acts was to join with his father in giving a site for Upton Church, and also an endowment. A few years later, when he succeeded to the baronetcy, he opened up the valley of Ellacombe for working men's dwellings, which have increased greatly beyond the modest limits he originally set. The central piece of ground, known as Ellacombe Green, was presented by him to the town on the occasion of his elder son attaining his*

The large mansion built overlooking the sea at Torquay

> *majority. The late Lord Haldon developed the resources of Torquay to a greater extent than it was possible for his predecessors to do. The greatest undertaking to which he set his hand, and which he carried out to a successful completion, was the building of the outer harbour, thus converting*

Torquay into one of the best yachting stations along the southern coast.

The inner harbour, which is six acres in extent, being too small and shallow to admit of the entrance in all weathers of vessels of any great size, a well considered scheme of constructing an outer harbour of ten acres in extent was decided upon, and the foundation stone of the new harbour and pier was laid, on September 6th 1867, by Miss Palk, his lordship's eldest daughter. The engineer was Mr J P Margary, and the architect Mr J W Rowell, and the works were carried out by Mr James Mountstephen. The cost of the whole undertaking was close upon £70,000. (Transactions Devonshire Association XV 1883)

When his son, Lawrence Hesketh, inherited in 1883, it was discovered just how much the estates were encumbered and that although the gross annual income was given as £109,275, very little of this was actually received.

It must have come as a great shock. Poor Lawrence Hesketh! Born to great expectations, brought up with a silver spoon in his mouth — elevated to the peerage — only to see it all melt away from him, with the final indignity of being delcared a bankrupt in 1893. A new mortgage had been drawn up with the Royal Exchange Assurance Corporation who had refused to accept repayment by the sale of small lots, but it made no difference. In 1886 and again in 1894 there were two great sales held by the Liquidation Estates Purchase Co. These were largely of the Torquay properties. Haldon itself was put up for sale in 1892.

The second Lord Haldon moved to London, where he died on Christmas Eve, 1903, after tumbling down the stairs. None of the Lawrence's lived to a great age. Sir Robert was 81 when he died, but his son was only 47, and his son, 53. The first Lord Haldon died aged 65, his son at 57, and the third and fourth Barons at 64 and 42 respectively.

On inheriting in 1903, the third Lord Haldon, Lawrence William, was declared bankrupt with liabilities of £500 and assets 'nil'. The last parcels of Palk land in Torquay were sold off and the family disappeared from the Devon scene completely. He had been educated at Eton, followed an Army career and was married to Lidiana Crezencia whose father had been an officer in the Russian Imperial Army. Their address was The Laurels, Elmes End Road, Beckenham, Kent. Their son, the Hon Lawrence Edward, was born in 1896, and succeeded in 1933.

The last Lord Haldon in the direct line was apparently a bad lot. At the age of 30, when he was described as working as a clerk, he was imprisoned for four months for forging his mother's signature to a cheque. He died in 1938 as a result of an operation, and in 1939 *The Times* carried an intriguing report that Lady Haldon of Stoke-on-Trent, widow of the 4th Lord Haldon, had given birth to a son, Lawrence Edward Broomfield Palk. *The Times* saw fit to add that the late Lord Haldon had at various times been a film extra, a cook on a cargo boat and a furniture salesman at Harrods. But all was not as it seemed. *The Times* further reported later that same year "that one Lizzie Ireland (alias Lady Haldon) aged 62, had been found guilty of conspiracy of concealing birth and various other charges. She had bought an unwanted baby and attempted to pass him off as the heir to the title. She was sentenced to three years penal servitude."

The title passed to a distant relative and then became extinct.

So much for the family. The name survives in and around Torquay but around the parishes of Dunchideock and Kenn there are no associations. High on the Haldon Hills, the newly restored Lawrence Castle is a lasting memorial to an extraordinary friendship, but even that is more usually called

Haldon Belvedere.

Unusually for a family of such prominence, there are no grandiose memorials to them in the church at Dunchideock. There are no memorials at all. General Lawrence is remembered with a large marble wall plaque and fulsome epitaph, next door to which is a simple tablet informing us that the remains of Sir Robert Palk, his infant daughter, Sir Lawrence and Sir Lawrence Vaughan were removed from the church and reinterred outside the west wall in 1892. The tablet was erected by their descendants in 1912. And outside the last resting place is a plot of grass surrounded by a simple granite kerb with just the single letter 'P'.

It is sad that so little evidence of the house has survived. Perhaps because of their catastrophic financial demise and complete removal from the county, few records have come to light of the Palk's long occupation of Haldon. The disgrace of bankruptcy seems to have drawn a veil over the very name of the family. No portrait or photograph of any of them exists in the county – no statues, no memorials.

Haldon House was a strange piece of architecture. A description of the house and its early history comes from Polwhele.

It is one of the best modern houses in Devonshire executed after the model of Buckingham House in St James's Park. Sir George Chudleigh died before building was completed. At his decease Haldon House consisted of four regular fronts, six rooms on each floor with suitable offices in separate wings. Haldon House was built of brick which Sir Robert Palk covered with Rawlinsons patent stucco – this gave it the appearance of a free standing stone structure.

There were formerly slopes and steps that led up to the hall door so that the offices below were underground. All this ascent Sir Robert Palk removed and laid open the offices by which the house appears one storey higher than before.

(In niches in the arcade are marble busts of Europe, Asia, Africa and America.) The great

Haldon as completed by Sir Robert Palk

front is eastwards. Two geometrical staircases, one at the north and the other at the south were lately erected. The gardens to the south side of the house were lately removed to some little distance by Sir Robert and their place is now occupied by lawn with suitable plantations.

Improvements around the house are happily planned and the rapid and vigorous growth of the many thousand trees which have been recently planted excites our surprise from the high and open situation where they flourish. Sir Robert Palk has by Act of Parliament enclosed some hundreds of acres from Haldon for the purpose of extending his plantations.

Polwhele writes that Sir George Chudleigh left the estate to his four daughters, the second of whom, Lady Chichester, inherited Haldon. She sold to Ann Bassett, who sold to John Jones, who sold to William Webber, who sold to Sir Robert Palk, so that it changed hands several times in a short space of time.

It would seem that John Jones was living there in 1765 when a faculty was granted to him for the erection of a pew in Dunchideock church.

An early painting of Haldon in 1780, by Francis Towne (Tate Gallery)

From the diaries of the Rev John Swete in 1792, comes this description of Hall Down.

We now traverse the Northern range of the Race Ground, and soon after arrival in view of Halldon House, the fine seat of Sir Robert Palk. This magnificent structure was erected by Sir George Chudleigh about 70 years ago, the plan of which he inconsiderately took from Buckingham House. I say inconsiderately for surely so it must be deemed by every observer who that had any prospect before him if he had any taste would endeavour to shut out that prospect? Who that was unconfined in extent of ground on either side of his house would bring forward his offices as wings in its very front, it might be expedient in a town but was absolutely ridiculous in the country.

...and had these wings, connected as they are by a corridor, been drawn up in the same line with the house, the whole would have been marked by a superior degree of grandeur and magnificence and it would have been exceeded by but few seats in the kingdom...

Sir Robert Palk has been in possession for upwards of 20 years. In that time, the hand of taste hath decided every improvement – 'twas that which removed the walks and fountains and the gardens which surrounded the house and converted them into lawns and 'twas that which made the formal vista give place to the more pleasing and less artificial clump.

The only description of the interior of this remarkable house, as the Palks knew it, comes from the 1892 sale catalogue. Polwhele has described how Sir Robert Palk removed the sloping ground from the front so that the original cellars and domestic offices appear as the ground floor, and all the principal rooms were at first floor level; because the house was built on rising ground these rooms would have been at ground level on the south west front.

The beautifully presented particulars give details of over 40 rooms.

Entrance is gained through a glass-fronted door opening into

THE ENTRANCE HALL,

49 feet long, the latter being inter-columniated with marble columns to carry the floor above, and from which a short flight of stone steps leads to

THE PRINCIPAL HALL

To the left of the Entrance Hall is

A BALL ROOM,

49 ft. by 17 ft. 6 in., which overlooks the carriage approach, the walls of which are recessed for seats and crowned with a decorated cornice; at the end of the Ball Room are two plate glass fronted Rockeries fitted with miniature fountains and lighted from above. To the right of the Entrance Hall is a Cloak Room, Water Closet, &c.

THE PRINCIPAL RECEPTION ROOMS

Are all on the ground floor, and the winding staircase from the Entrance Hall lands upon the

STONE GALLERY OR PRINCIPAL HALL.

This Hall is 50 feet long, and is decorated in keeping with the Staircase, which springs from here to the floor above, the walls being recessed for ornaments or miniature statuary, and the whole is lighted from above by means of a circular skylight. A door from this Hall opens on to the

BALCONY,

Which is guarded by ornamental balustrade and supported by the corridor beneath. This Balcony extends along the greater length of the advancing wings, and the side walls are relieved with classic columns and pilasters and stone statuary. To the left of the Stone Gallery is the

CHARMING DRAWING ROOM,

50 ft. 6 in. by 17 ft. 6 in., lighted with lofty windows at both ends, commanding most lovely views. This room is fitted with two carved marble fireplaces and at about half is partially divided by an ornamental flat arch carried by fluted pilasters; the upper sides of the arch and also the walls of the room are crowned with a chastely moulded cornice picked out in gilt. The door is surmounted by an elegantly carved pediment, the summit of the tympanum being broken to receive statuary. This room adjoins and communicates both with the Library and Dining Room.

THE LIBRARY,

34 ft. by 20 ft. 6 in., is lighted by heavy plate glass windows overlooking the pleasure grounds, and has also a plate glass panelled door opening on to the South Walk. It is a most perfect apartment; the walls all round are fitted with book shelves, and the four doors leading therefrom to the Dining Room, Drawing Room, Ladies' Boudoir and Lobby respectively, are all made to represent filled book shelves, so that when they are closed there is the appearance of books all round.

THE DINING ROOM

Is very handsome, and measures 30 ft. 9 in. by 21 ft. It overlooks the carriage approach and the park lands beyond, and is also fitted with extra doors leading to the Drawing Room and Justice Room, and has also a heavy plate glass panelled door opening on to the Balcony. It has a very fine statuary marble mantel piece, and the floor is inlaid with oak, the doorways have carved canopy heads, and are fitted with heavy polished mahogany doors.

THE JUSTICE ROOM,

20 ft. by 19 ft., is lighted by two lofty plate glass windows also overlooking the Park, and is fitted with a wide marble mantel piece.

Adjoining the Justice Room is

ANOTHER SMALL LIBRARY OR STUDY.

1919 sale catalogue

The ballroom must have been quite something, and in the very height of fashion. The range to the right (west) contained the 'batchelor wing' beyond which were the estate offices and the stables.

On the outside of each of the wings are two very imposing arched entrances leading to the Laundry and Stableyard, the arches being supported by Doric columns surmounted by a Frieze and balustrading.

The clock turret and bell tower and the private chapel "of very pleasant design erected at a cost of many thousands of pounds" are also mentioned.

The east wing contained the smoking room and extra bedrooms. Outside, there were the usual extensive kitchen gardens with their ranges of glass houses, potting sheds etc., and numerous outbuildings.

The price paid for this stateliest of stately homes is believed to have been £46,000.

The next recorded owner was James FitzGerald Bannatyne.

The Bannatynes were an Irish family, from Fanningstown, Co. Limerick. Mr Bannatyne had inherited the Limerick Milling Co, then operating at a considerable loss. However, he proved such an adept businessman that he was able to sell out at a considerable profit in the 1890's and set about realising a long-held ambition of purchasing an English country seat. Haldon Estate took his eye, and he and his wife Gertrude, his son and two daughters, moved in to take up their position among the English country gentry.

The Bannatynes made one major alteration which radically altered the appearance of the house. They put back the sloping ground in front of the house and constructed a double flight of stairs to a new central front door.

They appear to have been a popular family, and Haldon House enjoyed a brief interlude of prosperous, happy ownership. Photographs exist in several private albums showing beauti-

J F Bannatyne and his son, FitzGerald

August. 25.ᵗʰ - Sep: 2ʳᵈ
1906.
HALDON,
EXETER.

57

fully dressed ladies and gentlemen at parties, picnics, cricket matches and other jolly gatherings.

But it was not to last.

James Bannatyne died on 18 October, 1915. His son, also James FitzGerald, died of wounds on 14 May, 1916, and was buried at Merville, in France. Both are commemorated in Dunchideock church.

The obituary which appeared following the death of James Bannatyne Snr gives a pleasant description of him, and of life at Haldon in those closing years:

...died on 18th October, 1915, formerly principal of the Limerick Milling Co. He was 82, JP and Deputy Lt of the county of Limerick. He married Emily Gertrude, daughter of Mr Richard Bassett Wilson of Cliff Hall, Yorks. Open hearted to a degree, never an appeal for any worthy object was made to him in vain.

So generous was he to those who lived in the vicinity of the Haldon estate and the poor have lost in him a real friend. He didn't take a prominent part in local or county affairs but he was keenly interested in horticulture and was a regular exhibitor at the annual exhibitions held on the Haldon estate. He was a sportsman in the true sense of the word being particularly fond of cricket, evincing interest in the matches which took place on the estate. His eldest daughter married in July, 1911, Ludovick Heathcoat Amory.

The obituary does not mention James Bannatyne's interest in the new science of telegraphy. He was an enthusiastic supporter of Marconi, both financially and personally. Marconi was often a guest at Haldon, and there are local memories of a gardener's boy cutting down a clump of bamboos so that Marconi's apparatus could be set up, and it is even possible that one of the earliest transmissions was from Haldon Hill.

To Mrs Bannatyne, bereft of her husband and only son within a year, the upkeep of Haldon House

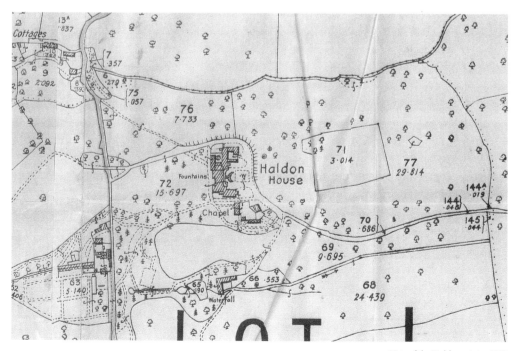

Map of the Haldon estate, 1919

must have seemed a pointless struggle. With one daughter married, there was only herself and her other daughter left, with all able-bodied menservants away at the war. The days of light-hearted picnics, of cricket matches and society balls must have seemed another world away. On Friday, 14th November, 1919, the Haldon Estate was offered for auction at the Rougemont Hotel, Exeter – and from then on it was downhill all the way.

The 1919 catalogue of the estate was a weighty, well-illustrated document of over 40 pages. The total acreage was 2,830 acres with a rental value of £3,548 5s 7d per annum, and it was to be offered first as one lot. If not sold, then in 16 lots. (There had been a sale of many of the estate farms the previous July, when, interestingly, the vendors were the Commercial Union Assurance Co Ltd.) Lot 1 was the "very fine residential and sporting property, Haldon House, with 1,040 acres", and listed as the last owner is T B Bolitho, esq. He was a brother-in-law of Mrs Bannatyne, and possibly the executor.

The house is described a lit-tle more exactly than in the 1892 catalogue. There is no reference to a ballroom, which from the dimensions would appear to have become the dining room; the library was unaltered with its book-lined walls and doors dis-guised as bookshelves. The Justice Room had become the Billiard Room, with bay win-dows and a door to the wide bal-cony "which extends along the whole front of the house and forms a distinctive and attractive

First Floor Balcony

feature of the house." On the first floor were 8 principal bed and dressing rooms and a "boudoir with a very fine panelled and moulded ceiling and marble fireplace, 2 bathrooms, one with showerbath, and WC. The bedrooms on each side of the corridor are all panelled and communicating. In the dressing room adjoining the boudoir is a telephone, and in Corridor are Speaking Tubes to Butler's pantry and to Second Floor nursery. Fire Hose and Iron ladder to roof." The Bannatynes had obviously brought Haldon up to date, and there is frequent reference to fire hoses, telephones and h & c water. Electric light was laid on to the entire house, stables and chapel.

There were a further 5 "good bedrooms, Bathroom and WC" in the bachelors wing over the garage, and there was a servants' wing with 7 bedrooms, sewing or linen room, box room, bathroom, WC. On the second floor were 3 nurseries, 4 good bedrooms, large bathroom, WC, housemaid's pantry, box room, coal room and a balcony at the end of the corridor. Again there was a fire hose in the corridor and staircase leading to the roof.

The Domestic Offices were all on the ground floor and were extensive, with a servants' hall, a lofty kitchen lit by a skylight, numerous sinks, larders, butler's pantry, flower room, and a Griffiths' wall safe. These rooms superceded the original domestic arrangements which were now classed as basement rooms and contained the former servants' hall, business room, wine and cyder cellars, butler's bed-room, brushing room, boot hall, wood and coal cellars (now outside in the backyard) and two boilers, one for hot water and one for the radiators "which can be used alternatively with the boiler in the stoke-hole in the back yard. Electric pump for pumping water from cisterns to the top of the house." The access to the basement was by four separate doors from ground level as well as two internal staircases.

Electric light was generated by a 25hp Hornsby oil engine in the timber yard with a 54 cell battery.

Outside were the pleasure grounds.

Then came the woods and plantations, which apart from their

The Pleasure Grounds

lie to the South of the Residence, from which a series of Winding Walks lead in various directions, bordered by a choice collection of Ornamental Trees and Shrubs brought from many parts of the world. Among others may be mentioned : Arbutus, Pinus Pinsapo, Evergreen Oak, Cork Trees, Abies Albertiana, Cedrus Deodara, Cupressi (including a fine specimen of the rare Deciduous Cyprus), Abies Douglasii, Hawk's Claw Maple, Variegated Oak, Weeping Ash, Willow and Beech, Tulip Tree, Schiadypytis or Umbrella Pine, Maidenhair Trees, Auriaefolia, Spirea, etc., and the mere presence of some, in their present flourishing condition, substantially confirms the reputed mildness of the climate. An attractive feature of the Grounds is a succession of Ornamental Pools, surrounded by Specimen Shrubs and Evergreens, the outlet from each forming a miniature Waterfall and terminating in a large Lake. The Lake and Ponds are stocked with Rainbow, Loch Leven and Brown Trout, specimens of which have been taken up to four pounds in weight.

beauty provided shelter from the winds and 'First-Rate Shooting'. The game bag for the three years prior to the War was stated as averaging 4,000 head including over 2,200 pheasants. In Haldon plantation to the south east of the tower (Haldon Belvedere) was a timber and thatched chalet with two rooms with fireplaces, used for luncheon parties in the shooting season.

A houseparty at Haldon

The cottages and houses on the estate seem to have been substantial, and built over a period of time in a variety of styles. The Laundry was half-timbered and thatched (consisting of a wash-house, with a range of tubs, copper boiler, wringer, copper cylinder and stove, ironing room with large stove, bedmangle and 2 large hot air cupboards with sliding clothes horses). The Bailiff's  House was built of stone with a slate roof and had 3 sitting rooms, kitchen, scullery, and 4 bedrooms, and was attached to a model dairy with a substantial range of buildings around two yards. This was the home farm.

Down the social scale came the cottages where the general rule was an outside WC or earth closet with a tap in the yard, or from a well, with rents varying from £10 per annum to £3 for the most primitive.

Included in Lot 1 was the timber, valued at £12,505, but not including certain ornamental timber. Elsewhere on the estate large areas of standing timber had previously been sold to the Government and were therefore excluded from the sale.

Photos taken of the Belevedere around this time show the hillside completely denuded of trees – what didn't go in the war effort presumably went to a timber merchant.

The conditions of sale contained two interesting clauses. The title to the property was to commence with "an Indenture dated 1st December 1897, being a conveyance in fee simple of the real property of the West of England Fire & Life Insurance Company to the Trustees of the West of England Fund of the Commercial Union Assurance Company Limited, and in part with a conveyance dated 3rd May, 1898." This would presumably be the date on which Mr Bannatyne became the owner. Clause 10 stated that parts of certain lots at one time formed part of the Haldon Family Estates and may be subject to certain charges. This condition appears in all subsequent sale catalogues until the final one in 1926.

The next sale is 21st April, 1922 and although the vendor is not named, it would be a fair assumption that Haldon had been bought by a timber merchant, possibly Bartlett & Co as they are mentioned later, for in 1922 the timber was specifically not included, and it was only "the site of such woodland" that was to be conveyed. The catalogue demonstrates all too plainly just how such estates were dealt with once the initial purchaser had completed his original purpose. The house was offered, still advertised as highly desirable, still well described and with the gardens, the chapel and part of the carriage drive. Lot 2 was the entrance lodge with 24 acres including part of the gardens and lake, lot 3 was the cricket ground and lawn, lot 5 was the Home Farm. Lot 7 was the 'Big Lawn and Front Lawn' adjoining the carriage drive, and lot 17 was Haldon Belvedere, with 30 acres. Once the estate had been divided in this way, it would have been almost impossible to attract a purchaser for the house. Another valuable asset was disposed of in 1920, by the same vendor, when he leased Haldon Common to the Forestry Commission for 999 years at an annual rent of £113 5s. This was then sold on in 1923 with the comment that the Commissioners were in course of planting the whole area, which in a few seasons would afford excellent game cover.

Written in the margin of the sale particulars is the comment that "Bartlett & Co were felling all the trees – saw mills at work in this area, wood cutting also being done, tree tops lying everywhere. Men continuously working hauling and cutting, this on the 62 acre compartment and three others." Written against the largest area of heath on offer, 250.344 acres, is 'not a single bird' and this is repeated against three other lots with 'not a bird since last season – one rabbit' against the last lots of brake and wood.

Haldon from the 1925 catalogue; the stucco rendering seems to have disappeared

The final attempt to sell Haldon as a "Residential and Agricultural Estate with a very fine Georgian mansion of moderate size" was in June 1925. The solicitors were a Cambridge firm, who continued to act until the final sale. The acreage had shrunk to 551 acres, and the estate was divided into 20 lots, including the Belvedere which must have failed to find a buyer in 1922. Lot 1, the mansion house, stables, chapel and 36 acres of pleasure grounds, was not sold. Lot 2 was the "very desirable market garden with a picturesque newly thatched house" which was still being run by the estate gardener. It included all the walled gardens, the orchard and the ranges of glasshouses. This was not sold either. Lot 3, the cricket field and front lawn, fetched £1,250; Haldon Lodge was sold for £1,150 and the purchaser was responsible for two tenths of the upkeep of the main carriage drive, but the ornate entrance gates and pillars were not included. The Belvedere went for £300 to A Lucas. On 29 September, 1925, a conveyance was made "between Frank Seaton Ingle of Bath Esq of one part and Vendor of the other part … part of the estate known as The Haldon Estate … free from incumbrances except an annuity by way of jointure of £2000 or less sum payable to Mary Constance Baroness Haldon during her life and also to a sum of £30,000 by way of portions for the younger children of the late Lawrence Hesketh Baron Haldon which sums therein referred to as the Haldon Family Charges…"

A year later a second conveyance was made between Herbert Moses Thomas of Boston Lincs, farmer (Vendor) and Ethel Mary Fry of 10 Ebrington Terrace, Alphington Road, Exeter, the wife of Ernest Fry of the same address, cattle dealer. What she had bought was 'the remaining portions of the Haldon Estate' offered on 26 March, 1926 'at Low Reserves to close the Estate'. There were still 237 acres. But the comfortable residence on offer was merely a wing of the recently demolished mansion.

A two day demolition sale held the previous September had sealed the fate of the 'fine Georgian mansion' which had stood empty ever since Mrs Bannatyne departed. Such sales always seemed to start in an unimportant upper floor bedroom, perhaps to warm up the bidding and wait for the late comers to arrive, and each room was sold in lots instead of offering all the doors, all the windows, etc. A catalogue survives with prices pencilled in against each lot – the upper floor bathroom 6ft enamelled porcelain bath with casing, lavatory basin and all lead pipes and taps fetched £4, the doors averaged around

10 shillings. A 35 foot run of moulded panelling in an upper bedroom made £16 10s, £25 in the next, £30 in the next, and £45 in bedroom 9. The white Sicilian marble chimney piece and hearth in Bedroom 10 made £40. The next 8 or so rooms are unmarked. Having disposed of all the deal flooring to the landing, corridor and all the bedrooms off, together with the skirtings where not otherwise lotted, the auctioneer moved onto the first floor landing. Someone bought 400ft of 3inch moulding, as fixed to the walls, 110ft of dado rail, and 150ft of picture rail. Did it all come off without splintering?

Fireplaces from the 1925 Demolition catalogue

Lot 147 was the well made stained pine staircase from the ground floor, with 26 treads and risers, 4ft 8in wide with 2 quarter landings, panelled spandril and doors, ornamental wrought iron balusters and mahogany handrail with 3 spiral ends. Unfortunately no price was given for this, but the stone staircase, 5ft wide with 27 treads – mostly winders with plain and ornamental wrought iron balusters and mahogany handrail only fetched 15 shillings.

The prices started to climb once the principal rooms were reached. The massive mahogany doors to the dining room, 7ft x 3ft by 1½in, with over-door, architraves both sides and fluted pilasters, fetched £42. The sash windows were 9ft high by 4ft 4in wide glazed in 2 squares, and with moulded and panelled shutters, carved architrave and mahogany seat with grill under – a bargain at £11. Excitement must have reached a peak when lot 194, was offered. This was the handsome white statuary marble chimney piece with Sienna marble fluted columns, frieze and alabaster relief, 7ft 7in wide by 5ft 9½in high and included the white marble hearth, a 26in dog grate with steel surround, iron panels and plate glass blower. It was eventually knocked down for £75.

The outer hall must have been a handsome room. The doors were of mahogany, either 6ft 8½in or 7ft high, six-panelled and moulded, and fetched £11 10s and £14 apiece. Two were described as 'in screen'. The door to the library had a carved overmantel, frieze and column pilasters and moulded and panelled linings – £42. Only £28 was bid for the pair of handsome 6-panelled mahogany doors with ebony mouldings, 9ft high by 7ft wide, by 2³/₈in, and a mere £7 for the pair 2in glazed and moulded mahogany entrance doors, 9ft high x 4ft 3in wide, with plate glass panels and deal shutters. The room was panelled and divided by a moulded, glazed and panelled deal screen 12ft 3in high, 10ft 3in long. The polished oak flooring to the hall and inner hall went for £35.

No-one was building large houses at that time, and after the savage depletions to the country's timber stocks caused by four years of war, it is inevitable that most of these lots were bought for salvage. One pair of those handsome mahogany doors can be seen, however, in the Imperial Hotel, Exeter. Most of the others were probably broken up. And so it went on, lot by lot, room by room, the windows detailed exactly, the doors, the marble fireplaces and the flooring. The drawing room contained a white enamelled china cabinet, 8ft 9in by 4ft 6in lined with cream velvet – ten guineas. The library fittings did not make as much as might have been expected. The doors fitted with dummy books that featured in the sale catalogues went for 20 shillings apiece, and 57ft of bookshelves for just £3, whilst the deal flooring made £22 8s.

Haldon had acquired a theatre; it makes a brief appearance in the 1919 catalogue as a playroom under the billiard room with a raised dais for theatricals. In the demolition catalogue it has its own corridor and lobby, and from the description of the windows was obviously in the basement and had probably been converted out of the original servants' hall. The windows here were mullions with sliding sashes and were probably original. Those in the main apartments may have been replacements from the Georgian originals with their much smaller panes of glass. The last lot inside the house was the lead pipes and radiators throughout the house (except in that part to be reserved) and the 2 galvanised cisterns on the main roof – worth £135.

The first lot to go under the hammer outside was Mr Bannatyne's new front staircase – of Portland stone with 39 treads and risers, 11ft 6in wide with two half landings, including the iron balusters and handrail, and also six solid stone vases with pedestals and the iron balustrading and stone plinth along the balcony. This fetched £40 – and where did it all go? Then came the 1½in York stone paving to the sunk garden in front of the stone steps "about 900ft sup." – £27, and the Portland stone paving laid under the balcony at basement level.

Adorning the front were four stone busts representing the four continents, sold in one lot for £57. Somebody paid £6 for the timber and thatched cricket pavilion, covered outside with sawn larch poles. And then, almost the final lot, came the piece de resistance – the ornamental wrought iron entrance gates, 11ft 3in high by 10ft 6in wide, including the two brick piers and ball finials. These look to have been of

1925 Demolition Catalogue

beautiful workmanship, and were sold for £90, the two side gates making £24, and it is to be hoped they were not bought for scrap.

The penultimate lot was the private chapel, which measured 54ft 10in by 17ft 10in and was described as a picturesque building constructed of stone with 11 beautiful stained glass windows, 16 seats in cedarwood, tiled floor to the aisle, marble floor and walls to the nave, and carved stone and marble altar. It was noted that the brass lectern and brass and marble memorials were excluded. No price is shown against it, so perhaps after the excitement of the gates our informant went home. Or it may be that the chapel did not sell. In the conditions, it was expected that it would be completley demolished – but the chapel is still standing, converted into a dwelling house. The chapel, which was capable of holding 100 people, was not consecrated, and was not part of the original Haldon House. As the Palks were buried in the parish church until 1860, this may be a clue to the date it was built. The absence of memorials to the Palks and Haldons either here or in Torquay could be explained by the 'brass and memorial tablets' reserved from the sale.

And then the final coup de grace.

Lot 424, The Remaining Fabric or Shell of the Mansion as it will stand after the Sale and removal of the fixtures and fittings … including:

The walls of the main building, the West Wing and a portion of the East Wing up to and including the Kitchen.

The whole of the Floor Joists (except in the Basement), Steel Joists, Girders, Beams, Roof

Principals and Joists to Flats.
The Iron Waterpipes.

The auctioneer mentions that he has other portions of the Haldon Estate for sale and in March, 1926, the final auction occurs. The demolition work had all been carried out, and what was left was the nucleus of the parkland, 237 acres, and the west wing of the mansion. This was described of 'modern construction soundly built of brick' and contained 11 bedrooms, 2 bathrooms, linen cupboard, three sitting rooms, the kitchen 19ft by 17ft with three sculleries, pantry, two larders with heavy marble shelving, all part of the original house, as were the 3 coal and coke cellars and the boiler for hot water. Across the courtyard were the stables, garage, coach house, loose boxes and living accommodation over.

The Georgian Haldon House had gone for ever, carried away on builders' lorries and scattered over numerous builders' yards. All that remained was the arched plinth that supported the main front, and one wing. The lodges and farmhouses, the chapel and the belvedere are all well preserved fragments of what was once a splendid whole, but of Haldon House itself, all that remains is a litter of sale catalogues.

Sources

Manuscripts from Mrs Bannatyne (D&E Institution)
Numerous sale catalogues lent by the late A Winkworth Esq.
Private sources

Shobrooke

THERE are still Shelleys at Shobrooke Park. Despite many ups and downs, many indirect successions, one rebuilding and one disastrous fire, the estate remains in the same family that bought it in the mid 1700's.

Until the 1840's the house itself was known as Little Fulford, supposedly to distinguish it from Great Fulford in the parish of Dunsford, but the manor was recorded in Domesday as Sotebroca with 354 acres, and it was one of many given to Robert, Count of Mortain, half brother to the Conqueror. The loser was Ordulph, son of the Duke of Devon.

The first recorded owner of importance was Sir William Perriam, an eminent judge, who became chief Baron of the Exchequer (and Mayor of Exeter), and who is remembered with an impressive monument in Crediton church. He purchased 'the estate of Fulford and Shewbrooke where he built a fine house whereon had been a mean habitation.'

From this it would seem that Shobrooke had been used purely as a farm. Sir William must have realised the potential of this tranquil site, within fairly easy reach of Exeter, and thus was the first owner to develop the estate.

The house at that time occupied a site, marked on the 1906 maps, at the lower end of the parkland – described by one source as midway between the long avenue and the sawmill. The avenue survives, of venerable old limes leading up the hill in stately procession to the church. To understand the layout of Shobrooke Park it is necessary to realise that the siting of the 19th century house has thrown much of the original layout out of focus.

I have already observed that it owed all its erection to Sir William Perriam who had purchased the estate from Robert Mallet of Wollegh. The judge had three wives by whom he had no male issue and on the estate being divided among his four daughters by one of whom it came to Basset, who sold it to Tuckfield whose place of residence prior to this purchase was Venny Tedburn, a village in the parish of Crediton. The first of this family was a clothier and established a large woollen manufactory which has ever since subsisted in these parts, acquired a considerable fortune. By an heiress of this family this and other estates were conveyed to Col Francis Fulford of Fulford in Dunsford parish. As this place is now called Little Fulford it is probable it acquired its diminutive epithet when the two Fulfords were the possession of one lord as was now the case in the person of Col Fulford … revert on the decease of the Col in 1700 to the Tuckfields, it has since that period continued in the family and the present proprietor is Henry Tuckfield. (Rev Swete 1790)

The house that the Fulford family occupied was described as partly of brick, and partly of stone, with good cellars and stabling for 27 horses – such were the priorities of those days! There was a 'Culverly'

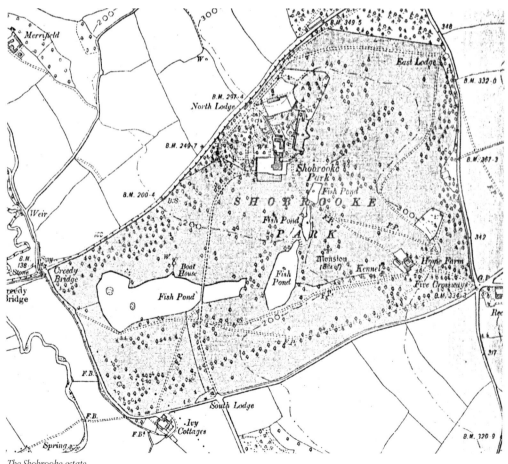

The Shobrooke estate

– a pleasure ground with a dovecot, with the River Creedy running through the meadows beyond. Following the death of the last Tuckfield in 1767/8, the property passed to the four daughters of a cousin, Mercy. However, the unmarried sister of Sir John continued to occupy Little Fulford until her death in 1807 aged 92. An attempt had been made to auction the property earlier and these sale particulars have left us with a description of the house. The hall had an "oaken staircase with Virginia walnut bannisters and a dado of yew at the head of which was a gallery 50 foot long and 9 1/2 feet wide." The dining room was elegantly stuccoed in gothic style and had a good chimney piece. The drawing room was somewhat smaller with a chimney piece of black marble, and the walls hung with green silk. Among others, there were a "green bedchamber, a settee bedchamber, and the chintz or sprig bedchamber, and Mrs Tuckfield's bedchamber." Either it was never offered for sale, or else it failed to find a buyer – perhaps old 'Mrs' Tuckfield, as she was known, refused to budge – and there she stayed for another 40 years.

The cousin was called Mercy and she married John Hippesley Coxe, through whom it passed to Richard Henry Hippesley, who assumed the name of Tuckfield. (Crediton, Major Venn 1955)

Richard Hippisley was born at Stow-on-the-Wold in 1774 and he married Charlotte, daughter of Sir John Mordaunt, Bt. He died in 1844 and his wife in 1848, and both are commemorated in Shobrooke Church.

The house of his ancestors, whom he could hardly have known, was not good enough for Richard. It was a time of great rebuilding and aggrandisement; the gentry were erecting new houses, or altering existing ones, all over the country and he must have seen examples of this around him in the Cotswolds. In 1815 Richard Hippisley Tuckfield moved up the hill, pulling down the old Elizabethan house and replacing it with a neat residence, constructed of brick and adorned with a modest portico. The architect was one Mr Donaldson.

He would appear to have taken a great interest in the estate, and must have taken back some of the parkland leased out. When he died in 1844, his batchelor brother, Henry, inherited.

The house after Henry Hippisley Tuckfield had completed his alterations

Henry continued his brother's work, turning his attention to the Park. But first almost immediately upon inheriting, he called in the architect, F R Lee, RA, to 'prettify' the house. The shape remained unaltered, but the two men redesigned the plain exterior and created a house of considerable distinction. It was encased in Portland stone, and given a balustraded parapet punctuated by stone urns. Little is known of Henry Hippisley Tuckfield, but he must have been possessed of considerable vision and excellent taste – and a long purse for it must all have been most costly.

An account from the Diaries of the Reverend John Swete written in 1789/90 gives a good description of the house in its transition stage and not, evidently, to the worthy cleric's taste:

"Crossing the river by a trim bridge as spruce and white as painting could make it, I came into a narrow field intervening between it and the shrubberies." Here he discovers 'a canal' which lay between the river and the house and was an impenetrable barrier. He then pompously decides that

there is something to be disapproved of in the modern alterations to the south front … I came on a spot from whence I had a picturesque view of the pleasure grounds in two fronts of the house, that on the southern side modern whilst on the other retained the style of the latter end of the 16th century on which it was built.

The style of architecture which had prevailed in the original building and which was now manifest in the front towards the west (seen at the same time as the other) had been altogether lost sight of, nor was a bow window thrust out in the face of the new part a pleasant object; as there is little Beauty in the one, so there was no harmony in the other. On the supposition that the alterations had been not so widely incongruous that the style of the old fabric and the three bridges seen from the lawn had not been so conspicuous, the place would have been of consequence and well worth observation. As a specimen of the architecture and gardening of former times of which indeed so enamoured have we been of late of rustick and untricked nature, there are now few vestiges extant.

In the nicely shaved lawn, however, diversified with shrubs and flowers, in the smooth and dry terrace walk, in the Arbours and shaded seats, I know not whether there are not appropriate comforts, which are more than equivalent to the throwing all around the house in one wide lawn and making it common by taking a road before the windows – the background was exceedingly handsome being formed by groves of ancient trees growing in the park which lay behind the house.

Passing from the field I came to Creedy bridge and was pleased to find that the face towards Sir John Davie's house was not white-washed.

Having completed the house, Henry began on the park, and in 1846 the whole estate was laid out, hedges removed, farmland reclaimed and the whole enclosed in a high deer fence. A chain of lakes was created. One major alteration was the realignment of the village road to the church which was pushed a considerable distance to the south, necessitating the provision of a new lodge. The magnificent ornamental iron gates came from the French International Exhibition of 1867, hung between a pair of richly ornamented pillars.

It was around this time that the house was renamed Shobrooke Park. There is a much repeated story that the name change came about because a coffin was erroneously delivered to Little Fulford, instead of Great Fulford – which is many miles the other side of Exeter – and that Henry was so upset

The gate piers at South Lodge

The ornate French gates at South Lodge

he decided there and then to change the name. It is just as likely, however, that after all the expense and rebuilding, Henry Hippisley Tuckfield wasn't going to be satisfied with his new estate being called 'Little' anything. Shobrooke Park had a much better sound to it, and it was the ancient name of the estate.

In the space of 40 years the two brothers had transformed Shobrooke. A minor Elizabethan house in an ancient deer park had been swept away, and in its place a house of the first elegance set in exactly the correct position to enjoy (and be admired from) its new surroundings.

The approach was carefully thought out. It was the fashion for drives to be as circuitous as practicable, taking in the best features of the parkland and giving the visitor the best possible view of the mansion at which they would shortly arrive. The quick, short route in from the nearest road was for the tradesmen. Carriages for Shobrooke entered at the new lodge. The

The listed bridge across one of the lakes

drive then crossed the largest lake on the delightful arched stone bridge (had Henry been to Stourhead, perhaps?) and climbed the hill with the house becoming ever more prominent on its broad terrace. Many of the trees that once graced the parkland have now disappeared, but it was clearly the intention that they should mask the house, and thus the visitor approached at an angle. The four lakes were formed by damming the small stream and 'appeared from the mansion like a river running through the park.'

The very substantial terracing on which Shobrooke sat and which gave it such prominence, bears some resemblance to that at nearby Creedy House, their closest neighbour – perhaps there was a little touch of not simply keeping up, but going several steps ahead? It is of heavily rusticated stone, imitating the basement storey so fashionable at that time.

The visitor passed between a further pair of ornamental gate pillars and swept across a broad forecourt to the entrance portico. The stables were reached via a ramp to the rear – well out of sight! The whole terrace area was enclosed by stone balustrading with a series of pillars and ornamental urns, all of fine quality.

Shobrooke Park when newly completed must have been a lovely sight, and the cause of much envy amongst its neighbours.

Gate piers and gates to the forecourt

On the death of Henry, Shobrooke passed to Sir John Shelley (9th Bt), whose father had married a Miss Hippisley, a cousin of the two brothers. Sir John was on his honeymoon when Henry died and on his return was given a truly feudal welcome, he and his bride being led from the station through floral arches and beflagged streets, escorted by his own troop of 40 yeomanry and his farm tenantry. It must have been most impressive. The year was 1880.

The Shelleys came from Sussex where they had once held a large estate at Michelgrove, near Arundel. The story goes that this was lost at cards to George IV, who in turn lost it to the Duke of Norfolk, who demolished the house but kept the stables.

The heyday of Shobrooke was shortlived. Large houses require large incomes and the Shobrooke estates were inadequate for such a burden. At one time their lands stretched from Posbury to Thorverton on the river Exe, but over the years it was gradually sold off leaving some 1500 acres around Shrobrooke. The family struggled on, through the First World War and the difficult times that followed. As Mrs Shelley recalled, there were few servants, no petrol, no electricity; everything had to be fetched from Crediton, and it became quite hopeless. Lady Shelley was a semi-invalid and coping with the vast house must have been daunting. In 1937 Shrobrooke was abandoned and the Shelleys moved down to Crediton. Lady Shelley died in 1953, after they had moved up to Shobrooke House (the former vicarage). Sir John remarried, and lived until March, 1976.

For two years the house remained empty, then a chance meeting between the headmaster of St Peter's Court school in Broadstairs, and Sir John Shelley, led to that school being evacuated to Shobrooke at the outbreak of war. Many of the paintings and the larger furniture were moved to the apparent safety of a store in Exeter; what remained was boarded up to protect it from the attention of enthusiastic small boys – and the school moved in.

Three generations of Shelleys

A description of the house as the boys would have known it comes from Mrs Shelley. The hall had a parquet floor with an inner hall from which a staircase rose, splitting into two at half-landing height. (It is worth noting from the plans that the only other staircase backed onto this one, a not uncommon feature in such houses but with dire consequences in the case of fire.) On the right of the hall was the sitting room which was used by the children. The library on the right was a large room, some 60 feet by 30 feet, lined with bookshelves which were boarded up. There was a dining room and study backing on to the gun room and there was a cupboard full of old newspapers. A passage led to the butler's pantry and the kitchens. On one side was the billiard room with a full size table. Upstairs were four or five large bedrooms, then the nursery wing over the kitchens. Mrs Shelley vividly remembers the large, cold kitchen, about 25 feet square with an old-fashioned Dover stove, and two 4-oven Agas. Below were at least four rooms in the cellars including the wine cellar – after the fire Mrs Shelley recalls large numbers of bottles, their labels all washed away and the contents ruined by the water. Rumour has it that a complete run of Punch magazine from the first issue was also lost. Although some of the furniture and best paintings went to Exeter, much remained at Shobrooke, but it made no difference, for the storerooms in Exeter were damaged in the blitz. All that the Shelley family have left is the smaller pieces that they took with them when they left in 1937.

> *A small boy ran more than a mile in his pyjamas through dark and bitter Devon lanes early yesterday to summon the Crediton fire brigade, when fire destroyed the war-time mansion home of St Peter's Court Preparatory School at Shobrooke Park (newspaper cutting).*

By the time the fire brigade arrived, slipping and sliding up the icy hill, it was too late. Two boys and a nurse lost their lives and five boys, and five adults were taken to hospital. The rest – nearly sixty boys and staff, escaped. Two of those boys have vivid recollections of that terrible night:

> *I got to Shobrooke in the Summer Term of 1943, so it was real war-time. St Peter's Court had been evacuated there from Broadstairs to be safe, which was to prove tragic and highly ironic.*

Shobrooke was a beautiful house, as I remember, idyllically set with a view descending to the bridge over the lake, which we crossed to play cricket and to go, in crocodile, to Church on Sundays.

Because there were insufficient loos for the number of boys (about 60, I suppose), we had to use Elsans, which were out the back in the stable stalls. Quaint would be a suitable euphemism.

We were very cut off by contemporary standards. We could not telephone our parents and they could not visit us, except very occasionally, because of the constraints of war. Most fathers were away in the armed services and mothers would have seemed antisocial doing something as 'self-ish' as making the long journey down to Devon just to see their son. The government's slogan, 'Is your journey really necessary?', glared disapprovingly from every hoarding and, with petrol rationing, it was not possible to drive. It did not seem odd to us in those days that we did not hear radio (then known as wireless). The high point of the week for me was when the headmaster's son, Charles – the deputy head – read aloud to us on Sunday evenings.

By contemporary standards our diet would have seemed a little ascetic. For instance, with rationing strictly in force, one would have about two boiled sweets per week – or the equivalent.

The house served well enough as a school, though a sort of Nissen hut was built outside to provide extra classrooms. A disadvantage, however, was that there was no electric light. The house had gas pipes built in throughout and we had gas lights in every room. Electricity was only for power points. There was, of course, no central heating, nor would we have expected it. Chilblains were a familiar feature of most schoolchildren's life in winter in those days.

It was surmised by the fire brigade that it was faulty insulation in the (old) wiring that caused sparking which had set fire to the gas. The gas pipes then served to conduct the fire until they

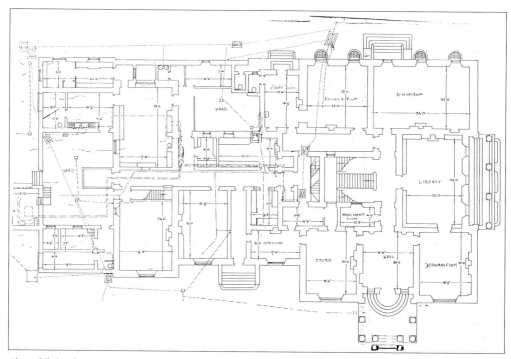

Plans of Shobrooke House

melted, for the whole (much panelled) house was completely ablaze with surprising speed.

There was a grand central staircase under a large glass cupola. I was one of about nine 10 year-old boys in a dormitory that gave off that central area and had a large Palladian type balcony outside the window.

The morning of the fire, a very few days after we had got back to school in January, we were woken in the middle of the night by the tinkle of broken glass. We supposed the noise was from a maid dropping the tray on which she took the headmaster his morning tea – and giggled. The dormitory captain (who must have been aged at least 12!) told us to 'shut up' and switched on his torch, which, to our horror, showed smoke billowing under our door. The noise had been the glass cupola breaking with the heat – and thereby creating a horribly effective draught.

We rushed out though the dormitory door and through the smoke raced to a doorway which gave towards the back of the house. We ran straight into a wall of fire and retreated rapidly to our dormitory. I had no eyebrows or eye lashes for weeks after!

We then climbed out through the window on to the large balcony, threw down mattresses, as it was a long way down, and then made a rope out of blankets. You can see how ten year olds would have thought them stronger than sheets.

Being heavy, the rope broke when I got to the first knot, so I fell the full distance and landed half on a mattress, which winded me completely. A boy called Cobbold kept saying 'Are you alive, Saxton?' and I had no breath to answer him.

Boys elsewhere fared differently. On the other main balcony was the headmaster and his wife, the Ridgeways, and they comforted the boys there until the fire brigade arrived and took them safely down fireladders. Others, particularly on the top, second, floor, were less lucky. Many jumped and received cruel injuries. In another part of the house, some staff members were cut off and killed.

Meanwhile, my group was safely on the ground. We were wearing only pyjamas and stood in several inches of snow, in bare feet. No-one noticed the cold.

It is difficult to describe the sheer horror of a big fire like that. The terrible noise is my most enduring memory. And the fearful (and I do mean 'fear-full') smell. So many different materials were burning. And great showers of sparks, which were actually small pieces of incandescent wood, exploded outwards like ghastly fireworks. One must have landed on my foot, though I did not notice the burn till morning.

A friend of mine, Richard Mercer, found a lad lying unconscious in the snow and carried him, intelligently, to the greenhouses. Unhappily, when he put him down, he saw the boy was dead.

We made our way to the gatehouse where we were kept warm until, early in the morning, we were taken to Crediton Grammar School, where the boys had been sent home so that we might borrow their dormitories. We were clothed by kind and much appreciated ladies from the WVS in Plymouth, who had clothes ready for people who lost their homes in the Blitz. The first time I wore jeans! The clothes had been given to the WVS by the Americans. (Anthony Saxton)

As for the dreadful fire I will tell you what I remember as it took place but, first of all, let me describe the circumstances that 1ed up to the event. We had not been back at school for very long and it was the first term that there was no night watchman on duty. Where the servants wing joined the main part of the house there was a store room in which all the boys' trunks were stored *during the term. Sometime during the night before the actual fire there occurred an electrical fault in this room which started a small fire and this was extinguished by a member of staff. However through the next day and*

evening the wind increased and during the following night this small fire was re-ignited by the draught. This then was the beginning of the inferno that followed.

The fire must have got going very quickly and, fanned by the wind, was soon out of control. The open staircase in the main building acted as a chimney which only added to the problem. My dormitory was situated half way down the servants wing and therefore not very far from the point where the fire started but, of course, another floor higher. We were woken quite soon by the smoke and going to the windows realised that they were all barred as were so many servants quarters in large houses. When needs must it is amazing what extra strength can be generated and we all got out by that route. I had on only my pyjamas and dressing gown with bedroom slippers on my feet. There must have been at least six inches of snow on the ground so you can imagine what state we were all in.

Looking down to the lakes, with the new Shobrooke to the right

Incidentally this fall of snow was responsible for the local wartime fire brigade being unable to climb the hill from Crediton because they had not got any chains. I remember well walking all the way around the house whether it was because I did not know what to do or because I wanted to see what was going on I cannot recall. It just so happened that, as I came round on to the main drive, the fire burst through the bell tower high up in the centre of the house and the bell came crashing down to the ground floor. I then walked further round until I came to the main back door at the end of the servants wing. It was then that out from this door ran a boy enveloped in flames and those of us there managed to put out the flames and I carried this boy up to the greenhouse where some people were gathering. This was Peter Charlesworth who was then taken to Exeter hospital where he later died. I think you can understand why I have vivid memories of that night. (Richard Mercer)

But it was the end of Shobrooke Park. The elegant house of the Hippisley brothers was a burnt-out ruin. A local builder salvaged what he could, then pushed the walls into the cellars and left a level, empty site. The stables and garages remain, tucked away in the shrubbery, and the beautiful parkland still delights the eye. A sailing club makes use of the largest of the lakes, and a public footpath leads up beneath the limes to the church. A recent Countryside Commission undertaking has helped the Shelleys reclaim the parkland. After half a century of neglect it had become very overgrown. Many of the mature trees came down in the severe gales of the 1990's and the rhododendrons and laurels had grown into jungles, seemingly impenetrable. But, with very little outside help, the Shelley family have brought most of it back under control. Large replanting schemes have been undertaken so that at least the parkland will once again look as it was planned.

Today the home of the Shelley's is more modest. Sitting on the edge of the parapet is a modern bungalow. To recreate anything remotely resembling the lost Shobrooke was out of the question, but the successor has all the benefits of the parkland, and none of the disadvantages of maintaining a large, unwieldy and costly house.

From the 1915 sale catalogue (Devon Library Services)

Marley

A stone built structure of great architectural taste and beauty in the Italian Renaissance style, The materials used were of the best description and no expense was spared in its construction, whilst the workmanship has left nothing to be desired. The decorations have been carried out in a princely manner, the walls and ceilings of the reception rooms being beautified by paintings by eminent artists. (12th September, 1905, Sale particulars)

So few traces of Marley House survive that it is hard to conjure up a picture of the large, ornate villa that once presided over 200 acres of wooded parkland bordering Lympstone Common. Almost all of the former pleasure grounds, orchards etc., have been built on, as the suburbs of Exmouth climb ever higher up the hill.

But, on closer inspection, evidences of the recent past emerge. One lodge and the entrance drives remain; parts of the stables and the outbuildings, the rides and ornamental trees, and on the site of the house itself sits a neat residence surrounded by some of the original balustrading and terracing that is all that is left of Marley House.

This was a sad example of short-lived wealth. Built in 1867 at unparalleled expense – arguably the most costly house ever to be built in Devon, lived in spasmodically by the owners for a few years only, let out until 1902, then abandoned and shut up; then put on the market for the first time in 1905.

After a succession of sales it all ended in 1930 when the contents and fabric of the house were sold. *The Exeter Flying Post* of 24th March, 1906 gives a good description:

The bare cost of erecting Marley House exceeded £40,000, and it was a job that everyone associated with it did well by. On this score the late Mr Luscombe was wont to confess that he had no cause to grumble. The late Mr Hitt, who at the time possessed a small carpentering shop upon the site of where the Co-operative Society's buildings now stand in St Sidwell's Street, undertook the joiner's work, which was all in Spanish mahogany save the domestic departments, which are of wainscot, and as a result of his savings at Marley he soon afterwards built a row of houses in Pennsylvania Road with the proceeds. Not being a particularly ambitious man, he lived in clover on the modest rentals they brought in, a retired and unassuming gentleman, for the rest of his life. Mr Harry Hems, who executed all the ornate and costly carved work, at its completion emerged from modest lodgings in Summerland Street and at once rented for himself a small house in Cox's Buildings, at the bottom of Paris Street, that being the first rung of the ladder he has since contrived to climb. The late Mr J H Parsons, of Grays Inn Road, London, who was entrusted with the ornamental plastering, declared afterwards that he had never had a better job in his life, and the late Mr Sang, the great German decorator who executed the splendid paintings there, thrived ever afterwards, and having lived to become one of the greatest specialists of decorative work perhaps in Europe, amassed much wealth, and died only the other day at an advanced age. As for the architect himself (the late Mr Benmore), he always declared he should never be satisfied until he drove into Exeter in his own carriage drawn by a pair of greys. He, too, was satisfied, for soon after Marley was completed his ambition in that respect was gratified.

Marley is built in the Italian style freely treated. The skyline of the edifice is effectively broken by a tower about 80 feet high standing directly behind the main porch on its south-eastern façade. The entrance leads immediately into a spacious hall 30 feet square, in which is the far-famed grand staircase constructed entirely of Carrara marble with hand rails of polished Ipplepen marble. Marble columns support the lantern above, the ceiling of which is profusely decorated with subject painting. These are generally supposed to be drawn upon the actual fabric; but they are not actually so. Sang really carried them out upon canvas and pasted and nailed them in situ after they had been executed downstairs. The drawing room faces the main front and overlooks the sea. It is 80 feet long.

The creation of this ornate pile was, according to *The Flying Post*, a combination of the talents of George Benmore of Exmouth, and E H Harbottle, FRIBA, the architect in charge of the restoration of Exeter Cathedral. Mr Benmore was the son of a small jobbing builder and it was his boast that he helped his father carry bricks up ladders when repairing the original house that stood on the site of the new Marley. The builder was Edwin Luscombe, who was also responsible for Exeter's Albert Memorial Museum.

There are few records of the original Marley Lodge. One account says that soon after 1785 a three-storey house called 'Whimsey' was built by an eccentric John Freston Scrivenor, who died in 1797 and left it to his nephew who renamed it 'Marley Lodge' – the field in which it stood was known as the Marles (*Book of Exmouth*, Robin Bush). By 1839 Whimsey had been rebuilt and was the property of James Winslow Phillips (*Memorials of Withycombe Raleigh*, M Williams 1945).

The only description of this earlier house comes from *The Flying Post*, 7 July 1831.

Marley Lodge near Exmouth, Devon. Messrs Hooper are instructed to offer for sale by Private Contract, Marley Lodge, together with its appropriate furniture and fixtures, and 54 acres of land, the present residence of its Proprietor the Hon Gen Brodrick. This Valuable Property is Fee-Simple and situated in the parishes of Withycombe and Lympstone, about 10 miles from Exeter, and 2 from Exmouth, commanding extensive views of the sea coast and of the River Exe. The scenery is strikingly beautiful and picturesque and presents to any gentleman requiring such an establishment an opportunity of possessing one of the most delightful residences in the county. The house comprises a Drawing Room 29ft by 15ft, Dining Room 23ft by 19ft, Morning Room 21ft by 15ft, Book Room 16ft by 15ft 6ins, Housekeeper's room 18ft by 3ft 6ins. On the first floor are five spacious bed rooms and 3 dressing rooms. On the second floor are 6 good bedrooms and 2 store rooms (there are three male servants' bedrooms, unconnected with the Principal House), 2 water closets, Butler's pantry, Kitchen, Servants' Hall, Laundry, Scullery, Brew House, Dairy larder, underground cellars and every other requisite office. The outhouses comprise 2 very excellent 4 stalled Stables, 1 single and 2 double Carriage houses, Saddle and Harness Room, with extensive lofts and granary over, a capital farm yard with Barn, Piggeries, Cattle sheds and Stables. The fruit and kitchen gardens are about 1^{1/2} acres which are inclosed and partly walled and stocked with trees selected by the present proprietor. There are about 10 acres of very fine Fir Plantation of long growth, a great portion of which are of Timber dimensions. The remainder of the property comprises the Lawn and Shrubberies, and 13 fields of pasture and arable land, the whole of which are in the highest state of cultivation. The property may be viewed between the hours of 2 and 5pm every day except Sunday by tickets only, which may be had of Messrs Hooper, 13 Paris Street, Exeter, of whom the price and other particulars of the property may be obtained.

According to *White's Directory* for 1850, Marley was the seat of Thomas Cobham, and would appear to be a substantial property.

It was not purchased by John Bryce until 1866, when the existing house was knocked down and work on the new Marley begun. Twenty years later *Morris's Directory* describes Marley, the seat of John Bryce, as "a magnificent mansion erected on the site of a former one and commanding one of the finest views in the county of Devon. The style is Italian with a sprinkling of classic and semi-Romanesque ornamentation and the interior is most artistically decorated both in sculpture and in fresco painting, the whole combining to form one of the most magnificent mansions in the west of England."

The outpouring of wealth was prodigious. It was reported that the furniture for the drawing room cost £38,000, though surely this must have included the marble embellishments, not just carpets, curtains etc. The life-size sculpture in the hall cost £2,000, and the grounds were similarly lavishly embellished with the sunken Italian gardens alone eating up £10,000. Even allowing for some exaggeration, the total estimated cost of half a million pounds cannot be far wrong.

Had Marley survived as it was built by the Bryces, it would have been hailed as a major example of its era, drawing together such an abundance of quality and sumptuousness as is hard to imagine. What possible use could have been found for it is another matter! Such houses, built as an expression of new-found wealth and in an attempt to establish the owners amongst the ranks of the gentry, were too grandiose to survive. Not only were they too large, but their owners rarely cared for them in the way that the old county families clung to their ancestral acres and usually more modest homes. To such people as the Bryces, their houses were built almost on a whim, treated with no more affection than a new dress – all the rage one moment, and banished to the back of the wardrobe the next.

The adjoining estate of Bystock was also owned and considerably altered by John Bryce and was not

Marley under construction

sold until 1906. One view is that he built Marley for his son and family.

The family was by all accounts cosmopolitan, and at the same time as Marley was being built, a similarly splendid mansion was under construction on the outskirts of Paris. They do not appear to have had a London address, and certainly no interest in their Scottish roots, nor do they appear to have mixed much with the local families, so that the name of Bryce is now more or less forgotten in the area.

But the family was as extraordinary as the house they built. What would seem to be a firsthand account of the founder of the family fortunes comes from the same article in *The Flying Post* of March, 1906.

And who was Mr Bryce, may be asked, the princely merchant who not only built Marley House in the 60's but also another grand mansion near Paris at the same time, remarking quietly, as the writer heard him do, that he was going to see who were the best builders – the English or the French. He was a typical Aberdeen man, tall and spare, but broad shouldered, who started life originally as an office clerk in a mercantile house in that Scottish city, and as a young man went out to South America upon being offered a vacant situation in a place of business in a city on the west coast. It was at Callao, if I remember rightly. Thrifty and untiring in his work, he contrived to save a little money. After being out there some years, an old hulk happened to be towed into the harbour. Now the port was constantly visited by many vessels, and stores of all kinds were always in demand, and as a heavy import duty was demanded by the Government, the prices of everything were proportionally high. Mr Bryce at that time happily conceived the idea of buying this old vessel, anchoring it outside the Customs boundaries, and stocking it with all sorts of necessities. These were delivered on board to him straight from the ships that were laden with his purchases, and hence, having never been landed, he contrived to procure them free of duty. This speculation proved a great success, for the captains of calling vessels naturally preferred to buy of him at reduced rates rather than obtain what was required at ruinous shore prices. Soon he became a prosperous man, and adding to his good fortune, this handsome young Scotsman in due course married a beautiful Spanish lady, whose father was a rich merchant resident there, and from whom at the latter's death he inherited immense wealth.

Then it was that he launched out largely. He practically became the owner of several of the Chincha and other guano islands, situated upon the coast of Peru, from which was obtained a manure then in great demand, not only in this country, but in many other parts of the world. To work these economically, he imported hundreds of coolies, who were shipped there by him at quite nominal wages under a seven-years contract and the promise of a bounty and a free voyage back at the expiration of their time. The result was that whilst yet in the prime of life, Mr John Bryce became a millionaire many times told. Returning to Great Britain, he bought the Marley estate in or about 1865 and soon afterwards built the mansion as already narrated. The stables in the rear were the first to be erected, and during much of the time the house itself was being built he lived a simple almost austere life in them by himself (the family being generally in Paris) attended by his faithful old housekeeper, Mrs Avis, who also resided there. A man of few words and rather reserved by nature, he seldom spoke, but would occupy his time by walking about, watching the while the workmen at their labours and continuously smoking huge cigars. When these latter were about three parts consumed, and when he thought no one observed him, he would throw the ends in among the rhododendrons and other bushes with which the grounds abounded. But this little weakness soon got known to many of the labourers employed, and at dinner time and other times they would hunt out the remains of the fragrant weeds, the smoking of which they afterwards greatly appreciated.

The late Mrs Bryce, being of noble Spanish blood, was naturally greatly interested in the Don Carlos movement, which at the time Marley was built was at its height in Spain. In furtherance of it, Mr Bryce, at his excellent spouse's suggestion, advanced immense sums of money in support of the cause, and it was understood that had Don Carlos secured the Spanish throne, the family's unstinting pecuniary assistance would have been rewarded by a Spanish dukedom. But things did not go as was then hoped and anticipated in the Peninsula, and so the rich owner of Marley died plain John Bryce after all, and not a Duke, as he might otherwise have been.

Although he was denied his Spanish title, old John Bryce would have been decidedly pleased to hear how his descendants prospered; two (great great granddaughters) are duchesses (English), and a third a marchionness. His son, John Pablo, and Maria Mercedes had six children. The eldest son, Paul John, took his own life in 1892, whilst an undergraduate at Oxford aged 20. A granddaughter, Janet Bryce, brought up in Bermuda and Canada, was married in 1960 to David, Marquess of Milford Haven, and is the mother of the current Marquess. Mary Mercedes, one of the daughters, married in 1906 Colonel John Phillips of Royston, Hertfordshire, and Sunningdale in Surrey. Their son, Harold Pedro Phillips, married Georgina Werner, heiress of Baron Wernher of Luton Hoo, and their daughters are the Duchesses of Abercorn, and of Westminster, and Lady Ramsey.

Charles, the eldest surviving son of John Pablo, had one son, Ivar. He was a great friend of Ian Fleming, the creator of James Bond and it is said that the character of 007 is based on Ivar. He wrote a book entitled *You Only Live Once* which is basically a biography of Fleming, but it gives us the family view of their beginnings:

My paternal great-grandfather was a Scottish lad who set out to make his fortune, and landed up

Mary (Bryce) and her husband Harold Philips

at the chief port of Peru, Callao, where he started a small ships' chandlers. In the 1850's, when old Bryce had worked up a modest business, Fate shook the dice and that unattractive, but oh so desirable, commodity guano was discovered to be deposited thirty feet thick on the entire surface of seven small islands just off the Peruvian coast. A miniature gold-rush followed. Sailing vessels of all shapes and sizes came homing in on Callao from the seven seas to join the queue waiting to load guano, an invaluable cargo. Their masts and stays and sails were worn and tattered, and the only ships' chandler for hundreds of miles was besieged with business.

Guano is the phosphate- and nitrate- rich deposit left by countless fish-eating birds over the centuries. There was no substitute for such a powerful fertilizer in those days, and the ships' chandler prospered accordingly. Overworked and without educated staff, great-grandfather sent an advertisement to The Times of London offering the position of book-keeper to any bright and adventurous youngster who would travel to Callao and apply. The months passed in the pressure of overwork, and he had almost forgotten the advertisement. The caller was small, dark and Celtic, and, producing the tattered clipping from The Times, announced that he would take the job, work the clock round and be an invaluable help to the old ships' chandler. There was a backlog of book-keeping as long as his arm, and my great grandfather welcomed him eagerly. 'You can start now, my boy. By the way, what is your name?'

'William Russell Grace,' replied the boy, and took over the pile of accounts. In a few years the business of John Bryce and Son became Bryce and Grace. In some more years, with my great-grandfather ageing, and with a fortune sent home to the Scottish banks and a son, John (my grandfather), a rich and popular young masher in Lima Society, he sold out on a deal to be paid for over ten years to his partner, W. R. Grace. Bryce retired to England and built himself a marble Victorian palace near Exmouth, christened Marley; while Grace, the genius, went on to build the shipping, banking and airline empire that dominates the business world of the South American Pacific Coast, W. R. Grace and Company. In the palatial boardroom of Grace in New York, there still hangs, or did until recently, a small oil painting of a ships' chandlers shop in Callao with 'John Bryce' painted on the shop front.

The younger John Bryce, my grandfather, stayed behind and fell in love with Mercedes, one of the two beautiful daughters of a temporary president of Peru, Manuel Candamo. The president was soon assassinated, deservedly I have no doubt, and his son aged eighteen and two daughters, seventeen and sixteen, were smuggled aboard a British ship by his friends, with many cases containing treasure, and went to Paris and the Ritz Hotel alive and naive. My great uncle Carlos, the eldest, and later to become Peruvian Minister to Paris, indeed eventually doyen of the diplomatic corps in Paris, grew afeared of the band of international ne'er-do-wells and fortune hunters who besieged his beautiful heiress sisters. So he bustled them off to Devonshire, where lived the only European family whom these homeless young Peruvians could count as friends. In Devonshire, Mercedes Candamo and John Bryce resumed their love and were married, to become the parents of four surviving sons and three daughters, of whom my father, Charles, was the eldest son. Though none of the Bryce or Candamo money lasted into my day, there was a great deal of it then, and they led wonderful, carefree and, I believe, also happy lives in those golden years. They were generous to a fault and were greatly liked by all who knew them. From the few old people I have met and talked with who were personal friends or servants, I have never heard a disparaging word.

Two stories of the pre-Devonshire period of these children's existence seem worth recounting. Mercedes (my Mamacita) told me how, as small children in Lima, they used to be sent down to their father's study in the evenings to be with him. He always said, 'My dears, I am busy. Just play quietly on the floor. Build walls and castles with all the pretty bricks in those boxes.' The boxes and cases were filled to the brim with gold coins, and they built whole cities of gold around the study walls, while their father was busy with his papers.

Again there is the story, widely believed in the family, of how my great-uncle Carlos, the eighteen-year-old boy, needed money to support them while in Paris. He had a letter, pressed upon him when they boarded the escape ship in Peru, and addressed 'To Whom It May Concern'. He took this across the Place Vendome from the Ritz to Morgan's Bank, I suppose, and joined the queue at a cashier's window. Under five feet in height, it took him a long time to reach the guichet, and even then he was waved back by the teller. 'Wait, sonny, can't you see I'm busy?' At last he was heard. He simply pushed the letter through. The clerk read it, read it again more slowly, then looked at Uncle Carlos, and asked him to come behind the barrier and wait in a chair for a while. Soon he returned with an important-looking gentleman who talked to him politely and asked questions about Peru. 'Well, my boy,' he finally said, 'how much money do you want? We will keep this letter for you while you are in Paris. It is an open letter of credit, drawn upon the Bank of England. I have never seen one before!'

That is the background of my father. He was brought up at a lovely country place, Bystock, near Exmouth, and went to school at Harrow, where he was a contemporary of Winston Churchill, whom he disliked. He was a remarkable athlete, a first-class player of all games, and devoted his adult life to shooting, fishing and golf, etc. He joined the Coldstream Guards, and fought in the Boer War. In 1914, he rejoined his regiment just in time to be sent with the ill-fated Naval Division. This was a new corps created by Churchill and consisted of sailors and marines commanded by Guards officers who crossed the Channel to land in Belgium and repel the Kaiser's invading army. Every man received a telegram 'Be at Dover by 4 pm today' and they were despatched to Ostend, from where they marched inland equipped with bicycle maps within twenty-four hours of the declaration of war. When the dark night came down, they bivouacked *and were awoken at dawn to find a ring of grey green uniforms with rifles aimed at them all around. They were captured, having lost their way in the dark, but by the neutral Dutch, not the German invaders of Belgium. They were interned – not as prisoners of war – in Holland for four years until released at the Armistice. My father fell in love with a Dutch lady during the intern-ment and he never came back to my mother and me. He returned to Devonshire again, this time to Westward Ho, and died there at the age of eighty-one.*

Although Ivar Bryce states in the introduction that his memory is poor, and there may be inaccura-cies, it makes fascinating reading.

For a house of such magnificence and of relatively modern date, there is a strange dearth of pho-tographs. Even the sale catalogues were illustrated only by the pictures of the hall. But these give the only descriptions available of the interior of this ornate villa.

The earliest sale catalogue to survive was dated September 12th, 1905, when the vendor was Mrs Mercedes Bryce. From this we gain a fair idea of what it must have been like.

The drawing room was a massive 71ft by 32ft with three bays, each having a fireplace with marble mantelpiece. The dining room was 31ft by 23ft with an alcove with marble columns. The morning room was a modest 25ft by 20ft and overlooked the carriage drive, and communicated with a fitted bathroom with lavatory and WC. In the billiard room, 26ft by 20ft, were eight stone staddles let into the floor to receive the legs of the billiard table.

The library (32ft by 23ft) sounds interesting; the bookcases were so constructed that it was impossible to see the joins in the bookcase doors, and the whole looked like panelling. Pictures of William Shakespeare, Sir Walter Scott, Robert Burns and John Milton decorated the ceiling – and were said to be very good likenesses!

But it was the hall that caused the most excitement. It would have cre-ated a stir wherever it had been built, but for such a display of opulence to be found in south Devon was amaz-ing. It must have been the talk of the area, and caused a sensation when viewed for the first time. Perhaps it was modelled on staircases that Mr Bryce had seen on his travels; per-haps he wanted to outbuild and out-decorate everyone else in the neigh-bourhood, in which he certainly suc-ceeded.

The bald details from the sale cat-

The fabled marble hall (Devon Library Services)

...*and staircase*

alogue state it was 42ft wide, 40ft high, and had a specially constructed floor of 40,000 Italian tiles. There was a life-size sculpture, of what we are not told, that alone cost £2,000. And then there was the staircase, illustrated by two photographs, which show how truly fantastic it was.

Magnificent marble staircase, the whole being elaborately executed in polished marble of rare selection having solid Sicilian treads with polished soffits. It is protected by ornamental balustrading with richly moulded Devonshire handrail supported by massive Cornish newels and conducts to:

the landing has a tiled floor and marble balustrades broken by 16 noble Ipplepen columns.

There were eleven best bedrooms with dressing rooms, all fitted with marble fireplaces, excepting two of the dressing rooms. The eight secondary bedrooms had to make do with marble mantelshelves to their fireplaces. There was one bathroom. On the second floor were eight servants' bedrooms.

The tower, which is gained by an iron spiral staircase, contains a capital smoke room having three windows commanding extensive views embracing the valley of the estuary of the Exe with the Haldon hills in the distance, magnificent stretches of the Channel and the South Devon coast together with the range of Dartmoor tors in the background.

Under the floor in the tower was a two inch thick slate rain water tank holding 4,000 gallons.

All the doors, including those in the servants' quarters, were of polished wood.

The whole massive pile sat on an "imposing ornamental tiled terrace with massive balustrading leading to two flights of broad steps".

The basement was described as "extensive with cellarage for binned wine, beer, wall cellars, etc." The out offices partly surrounded a large tiled yard and comprised a boot house, splendid dairy with tiled dado and marble benches, commodious storeroom, laundry, drying rooms, bakehouse with ovens and furnace, coal and coke store, carpenters shop and servants' bathroom. There were a pump house, dog kennels and superior stabling. Horses obviously played an important part in the lives of the Bryce family, for one unusual feature that is marked on the maps, and is still evident, was a sunken exercise ring beside the drive.

The kitchen gardens were constructed on the same grandiose scale. The vinery was 100ft by 12ft

6in, the curing melon and pineapple house was of similar size, the banana house was smaller and there were a 'span roof green house' and a three-quarter span roof house, both of around 60ft. The peach and rose house was a massive 166ft by 16ft 9in. Outside were tennis and archery grounds and a large aviary. Water came from the Bystock ponds up on Lympstone Common, built to supply both Bystock and Marley.

Part of the library ceiling (Devon Library Services)

It does all sound just a little bit opulent – and maybe that was the problem. The Bryce family do not figure largely in the county scene. John Bryce became a JP and High Sherriff, but the name of Bryce does not crop up amongst the social gatherings of the day, nor did they intermarry with any of the old families. In fact, they don't seem to have liked their new mansion very much at all. It is popularly stated that they never lived there properly, and the only time it was used as they intended was when a ball was held, largely on the terrace. One account states that the family spent most of their time abroad, and let Marley, which was said to take around 28 servants to run when lived in properly. Whatever the reasons, in 1875, just five years after his marble palace was completed,

An ornate plasterwork ceiling (Devon Library Services)

The Marley estate

John Bryce decided to reduce his staff, and turned most of them off, including his trusted coachman Henry Down, who had been used to travelling abroad ahead of the family to book accommodation and horses. Apparently the Bryce coach was in keeping with the house and is said to have had a coat of arms emblazoned on the panels, was lined with silk and had brass and gold fittings, and was painted in the family's colours of emerald and vermillion with gold stripes.

The *Post Office Directory* for 1886 lists John Bryce, JP, as the occupant of Marley Lodge, but in 1890, although he is still listed as the owner, the property was let to Walter Dunlop, and described as standing on a commodious eminence, encompased by ornamental shrubberies, sylvan walks and extensive grounds. By 1923 the directory omits all mention of Marley Lodge, and presumably its sad decline had irrevocably begun.

Although John Pablo never appreciated his home, it is good to know that it was lived in properly for a time, and that the gardens achieved some degree of fame. A long and glowing description of Marley in its short-lived days of glory was given in *The Gardening World* of December, 1894.

Marley Hall, the seat of J. Forbes, Esq., is beautifully situated on rising ground about two miles from Exmouth, and commands some fine views of the River Exe and its estuary, besides an extensive stretch of the South Devon Coast reaching from Starcross to Berry Head. On the opposite side of the river, the Halden Hills rise in all their beauty, and several fine establishments nestled among the hills can easily be discerned, Powderham Castle, the seat of the Earl of Devon, Mamhead, the residence of Sir L. Newman, Bart., being very conspicuous. In easy reach of Marley on the east side of the river are the fine gardens of Bicton; Nutwell Court, Lady Drake, Tarrington House, long time famous for its pines and peaches, whilst immediately joining Marley is Bystock, the seat of J. P. Bryce, Esq., with its extensive woods and preserves, magnificent rockeries, and well-kept glass erections, and pleasure grounds.

The approach to Marley Hall is by a well-kept drive, on the grass turf on either side being splendid specimens of choice conifers. In fact some twenty five years ago when Messrs. Luscombe, Pince & Co, had the laying-out of the grounds no expense was spared, and so now many of the shrubs and trees which have made magnificent growth are at their best. The Araucarias, Abies, Wellingtonias, Picea, and Thujopsis are numerous and well proportioned, whilst noble deciduous trees as single specimens on the wide lawns have their lower branches down to the ground, and give a richness and charm that wondrously enhances a wide domain. A wide terrace adjoins the mansion and at regular distances vases are fixed which are filled with good forms of bedding plants, the outer edges having large quantities of lobelia and Ivy-leaved Pelargoniums hanging over them. This large terrace, which is paved with fancy tiles, can be covered over, and when large parties were held in days gone by, made a grand addition as a promenade for the company without interference from unpropitious weather.

The Hall is a fine stone structure very substantial and imposing, giving one the idea of durability, strength, and proportion; the inside of the Hall, however, is par excellence that for which Marley is famous. The entrance hall, marble staircase and landings, the magnificent lower rooms, including the drawing-room, with its white marble columns being such as are seldom met with, and must be seen to be duly appreciated. On the lawn in near proximity to the entrance hall are two basket beds, some 14 or 15ft in diameter, the wire edge clothed with Ivy, and the over-arching wire covered with flowering climbers, these beds have been filled with flowering Begonias, one having pink flowers, the other crimson, and grand they have been. Whilst Pelargoniums, etc., have repeatedly lost their beauty through constant rain, these have always been gay, and the admiration of all who have seen them. The whole of the plants are seedlings raised by Mr. D. Moiest brought on in gentle heat, during the spring, and planted out late in May or early in June. I may say that I have never seen Begonias do so well as here, the flowers are broad and massive in every part, many almost circular, measuring 6in across, the colours most vivid, and foliage stout and dwarf; truly a fine strain.

Close by is the oval-shaped sunk flower garden whose sloping grass sides give a freshness and charm in keeping with the other choice portions. In the centre, ends, and on each side of the stone steps leading down to it are large vases filled with the usual flowering bedding plants, etc., whilst the beds which are some 8ft. wide, have choice herbaceous plants in the centre, and rows of self-coloured Begonias running all round, edged with Lobelia and yellow Pyrethrum. Two thousand Begonias in all are planted out so that some idea of the beauty of this can be imagined.

Passing from this lovely spot and through a piece of shrubbery we enter the kitchen garden, the principal entrance, however, into this part is by the frame yard at the lower end. A range of peach houses at the north end, 160ft long occupies a portion of the space, the remainder at this end and the three other sides have walls some 10ft. high covered mostly with pears, plums, and choice currant trees, the centre walk has a border of herbaceous plants, carnations being grown in large quantities. Long rows of Sweet Peas are close by, one of these being the pure white form, it being an essential that white flowers are always used in the decoration of the lower rooms of the Mansion. At times this is a heavy task, the family mostly being in residence. Peaches in the range do well, and fine crops have been gathered this season. In this range are grown the Souvenir d'la Malmaison Carnation for which Mr. Moiest is noted. Another good thing done here are the Marguerite Carnations sown in spring in a little warmth, planted out in the borders then about September, lifted and put in boxes, and abundance of flowers may be had for three or four months following.

In the frame yard are melon and tomato houses, etc., in this range is the most floriferous plant of Stephanotis I have seen for some twenty years; one previously being at Abney Hall, near Manchester, where Mr. MacKellar used to cut such abundance, and perhaps does still. Gloxinias are grown by hundreds here, the pure white Her Majesty being an especial favourite, flowers of this are still being cut and have been since May, whilst a fresh batch of bulbs are potted up, growing well, and will, early in the New Year, begin to give a quantity of this most acceptable form. Mr. Moiest is specially successful with these, and recently gave an interesting paper on their culture at the Exmouth Gardeners' Society, which was much appreciated.

Another kitchen garden neatly contains the range of Vineries, 90ft. long in three divisions, well built, and heated in Week's best style. Good crops of fruit have been gathered, the object being to get abundance of fair-sized bunches, well coloured, without any pretence to enormous, and often less useful clusters. Here we noticed large numbers of choice white Chrysanthemums – fine blooms of leading sorts. The Pine Stoves, 90ft long in three divisions are full. Some three to four dozen Queens and Smooth Cayennes are in various stages of ripening, and many fruits reach 5 and 6lb. The succession house is full of stout plants, whilst suckers are constantly taken and pushed on. A house entirely devoted to Bananas is a great success a number of immense clusters having been cut this season. In a large greenhouse near are quantities of Arum Lilies, and Marguerite Daisies whilst on the roof are masses of the White Swainsonia that has long been a mass of bloom. Many other objects of interest might be mentioned, but this will give some idea of the charm of this well-kept garden, which reflects great credit on the tact, method and perseverance of the painstaking gardener.

Considerable confusion has arisen over the years, not helped by the common christian name of father and son, and the insertion of a middle name, variously Pablo or Paul. John Bryce senior, who was the original purchaser of both Bystock and Marley, died aged 70 in Biarritz, and was buried in the private burial ground at St Johns in the Wilderness on 17th July, 1888. His is the only entry in the parish records, yet there are certainly four and possibly five graves.

The Bryces were catholics, and it is the catholic church that has the burial entries for Paul John Bryce, died 5th October, 1892 aged 20; buried 10th October; his father, John Paul Bryce, died 3rd March 1901 aged 54, and was buried 28th January, 1902. His tombstone bears the name of John Pablo. The last entry is for Maria Mercedes Candamo Bryce, who died in Biarritz on 16th May 1929, aged 80. Perhaps the second Bryce house was in Biarritz, and not Paris as given in *The Flying Post*.

This quiet, unkempt burial ground is the only lasting memorial to this extraordinary family. Their estate is almost entirely built over and the pattern of roads has been altered to accommodate the vast new housing estates. Fragments of estate walls, lodge houses and gate posts give clues – and all that remains are the neglected, crumbling marble tombs.

Although Marley was offered for sale in 1905, there is no record of it being bought, and it was again put on the market by Savills of London on 15th July, 1919. All the original deeds of the estate were lost in the blitz, so it is difficult to trace the succession of owners. But the next sale was 28th February, 1928 when the estate was bought by Frederick Woodgates for £11,000. Two years later he sold the mansion and five acres to R A Dagnall, a haulage contractor, for £4,000.

In June the same year, 1930, an intriguing paragraph appeared in *The Exmouth Journal*, stating that the whole of the exterior and the most valuable part of the interior, including the ceilings and the staircase, had been acquired by the principal of Uphill School for Girls, Weston-super-Mare.

Uphill School no longer exists, but it must have had extraordinary pretentions. Marley, with all its opulent marble fittings, could hardly be said to be suitable premises for a girls' school! If there was any substance in the report, then perhaps the principal discovered there were more obstacles than she had envisaged in transporting a house of this size all the way to Weston-super-Mare.

On 9th July, the site only of Marley was bought by a local estate agent, J E Brooks, for £510, with the vendor reserving the right to remove the fabric of the building over the next two years.

Mr Dagnell, who came from Canterbury, without any compunction whatsoever, decided to make what he could from the house and the following account appeared in *The Western Times* dated 6th June, 1930.

Noted Exmouth Mansion; Marley Fabric submitted at auction; some valuable marbles.

The house has some of the finest Italian work to be found in the west of England – one of the chief features being the grand staircase elaborately executed in highly polished marble of a very rare selection having solid Sicilian treads, ornamental well carved balustrading in three colours with richly moulded Devonshire handrail supported by massive Cornish newels with heavy caps.

The property was recently acquired by a firm of London contractors who have decided to demolish the whole block of buildings and to dispose of the land as a freehold building site. This despite the great interest shown in Marley by possible purchasers, including the Royal Family.

Mr Cecil C Cadle FNAA conducted the sale of the various fixtures and fittings which included 40 heavily moulded Spanish mahogany six-panelled doors and frames, 2 large moulded oak doors and frames, 40 mahogany frame sash windows with panelled shutters, 50 oak moulded window and sash frames, 42 highly polished marble Ipplepen columns with carved caps, several finely carved white Italian marble chimney pieces, mahogany library panelling, shelving, secretaire, black and grey Italian marble mantelpieces, a pair of bronze statues representing Venus, ornamental garden vases, etc. A start was made at 11.00 with the more unimportant portions in the boot hall, laundry and servants' quarters. The first lot, a 2in solid deal door fetched 10/- and a 222ft run of stone paving 12/-.

Further details were given in *The Exmouth Journal* which stated that a Mr T Rowsell, who had helped to build Marley, was amongst those present at the sale, which was held in the shade of the copper beech at the entrance to the house. The fabric of the house was sold for £3,500, the site fetched £510, and the lead was sold for £17 0s 6d per ton, despite a telephone bid from London for the whole lot at £17 per ton!

The sale took place on 3rd, 4th and 5th June, and there were 700 lots. Everything that could be sold, was, from the Italian flooring to the brass door hinges, the bricks from the walled gardens and even the turf from the lawns.

Truly it had all been a nine day wonder.

The only surviving fragment – the arch leading to the stables

Silverton Park, c1895.

Silverton

Silverton was a sad house. It was built by a middle-aged man, childless, who died before it was finished. From then on it became a complete white elephant, never finished internally, never properly lived in, and known locally as 'Egremont's Folly'. The ageing widow spent just a few months of each year at Silverton and it could never have known the life and laughter that should have filled its many rooms. It was not to see the great functions for which its builder had created such splendour, nor was it the hub of the community as was usual with such houses. Silverton seems never to have been much more than just a shell.

What we would have thought of such a house had it survived is an intriguing question. Would it have been considered worthy of Grade II* listing – or would it have been dismissed as an architectural freak, a hotchpotch with no real style or dignity, fit only to degenerate into institutional use, or at the best an hotel? We shall never know, for Silverton Park was demolished – 'blown up by grandfather sometime before 1914', according to the Wyndhams.

The countess of Egremont died in 1876; a furniture sale was held in 1892 – and that was that. If there was ever a demolition sale, no records of it have come to light. On 27th May, 1915, the Silverton Park Estate was offered for sale on behalf of Mr W. Wyndham of Dinton Hall, Wilton in Wiltshire, who had succeeded to the estates of the late Lord Egremont on the death of his own father the previous year. Lot 10, the site of Silverton Park, was sold privately for an undisclosed sum.

The quiet fields tell their own story. A row of stately limes crosses them, seemingly without purpose. A large magnolia tree stands stranded in the middle of ploughed earth. In a small copse there is a deep pond with a dam across one end. Now only a muddy trickle, it would have been capable of providing a large reservoir of fresh water.

The site of the house is totally overgrown. Elder and hawthorn, a few sycamores, brambles and nettles cover all that remains of 'Egremont's Folly', daffodils marking the grave of a once great house. The holly shown in the last photograph taken before it was demolished is there still, windblown and in decay, but marking the spot where the front terminated. Rabbits have made holes in the earth and run riot in the cellars; here and there the arches that once supported the great weight of the mansion are exposed, fragments of columns, of the friezes and other debris, are embedded in the nettles. The outlines of the platform at the front are clear, some of the brickwork still in situ. A round outline beneath a tree root turns out to be part of a brick column. The woodland behind the house is neglected, overgrown and haunted with the everlasting cawing of rooks.

Bramley Park, Surrey

Silverton Park has been described as a 'Greco-Lilliputian extravaganza'. Certainly the Westcountry has never seen its like before or since. The architect of this wedding cake of a house was James Thomas Knowles, an up-and-coming young builder turned architect from Reigate in Surrey. Captain Wyndham's residence, before succeeding as 4th Earl of Egremont, was at Bramley Park, near Guildford, which remained an unpretentious small house until 1837, when he rebuilt it as 'a noble erection of Brick and Slate, covered with Metallic Cement, in imitation of Stone … and on either side a long Colonnade.' This is the house which became the childhood home of Gertrude Jekyll, and it, too, has now gone, demolished in 1951. It would seem that elements of both Bramley, and the incredible design for Egremont Castle at Orchard Wyndham (an earlier design also by Knowles) were combined at Silverton. Stripped of all the colonnades and accretions, it was basically a square house of not unreasonable proportions, and was just that, for Knowles was adapting an existing building. Architecturally it was already moving out of fashion; the love of all things classical inspired by the many who undertook the 'Grand Tour' was waning and new fashions were

A sketch dated 1879 (Exeter City Library)

soon to sweep away this style. At Silverton, 'Corinthian columns sit on Ionic; Thrasyllan pedestals crown the corners – perhaps waiting for an ornamentation of statues or urns, and round the upper storey ran a frieze executed in the classical style, but telling the story of the passage of Israelites through the Red Sea.' (Priscilla Metcalf, *The Country Seat*, Penguin 1970)

The fourth, and last, Earl of Egremont was consumed with a passion for building in the very grandest of styles and, in common with many of his contemporaries, his ideas of what was due to his position and style outran his estate's ability to pay.

There seems little doubt that had the earl lived he would have had to sell the prodigy of his outlandish taste and settle for a modest style of living.

This description of the earl and his activities is given by the Rev Chalk, writing in the Devonshire Association's *Transactions* in 1910, some 65 years after the death of his subject.

On the succession of George Wyndham, 4th Earl of Egremont, on 11th November, 1837, to his uncle's title and estates, a new and disturbing influence was felt from which our community has not recovered. The new peer was born on 6th October 1786, and married on 14th November, 1820, the third daughter of the Rev William Roberts, Vice Provost of Eton. The great part of the earl's estates passed to the natural children of his predecessor and he appears to have been seized with a desire to emulate the opulence and importance of his cousins. In consequence, the eight years of his earldom were years of the most frantic profusion. He built the large mansions of Silverton and Blackborough, the bridge at Kentisbeare, the rectory at Silverton and part of that at Kentisbeare and the whole of Blackborough church. In addition he collected furniture and paintings without regard to cost. His steward, a barrister commonly called Counsellor Tripp, discovered that the village of Kentisbeare and large Somerset property had been let on lives by faulty leases. These he proceeded to recall with the result that great distress was felt in the village and some were even ruined. This spendthrift consumed £300,000 in eight years and the estates are still encumbered with mortgages.

In fact it took his heirs until the late 1970's to clear those mortgages, and the total of Practical Debt on Estate was £251,070, borrowed from several Wyndhams and other noble relations and friends – all private debts. Between 1863 and 1869, £73,700 was paid off with interest at 5%, but a further £38,000 was borrowed. It cost over £10,000 per annum in interest alone.

It has been said that in designing Silverton, and Egremont Castle at Orchard Wyndham before it, the earl had sought to rival Petworth House in Sussex, the ancestral home of the Percy and Wyndham families. The family history at this point is somewhat complicated – and irregular. The third earl was a man of generous tastes and it was said of him that in his lifetime he 'lent' over one million pounds to relatives and friends in need. He was originally engaged to be married to Maria Waldegrave, whose mother was the Duchess of Gloucester and therefore of Royal blood. However, the earl was a plain young man and the thought of allying himself to the Royal House apparently gave him serious cold feet and the wedding was called off – around 1785. In complete contrast some five years later he formed an alliance with a girl of humble birth, Elizabeth Ilive. She moved into Petworth as 'Mrs Wyndham' where she bore the earl three sons and three daughters, all out of wedlock. Did the local gentry receive her, or was she cold-shouldered by the neighbouring ladies, and could this have been a contributing factor to the earl's belated decision to make an honest woman of the mother of his sons? In 1801 they married. In 1803 a Deed of Separation was drawn up and she moved out of Petworth! It would seem the rise in her status to Countess proved too much and their cosy relationship was at an end. The result of this was that although Elizabeth's children could inherit all their father's wealth and unentailed property, the title was denied them.

The heir to the earldom was the son of the third earl's youngest brother, the Hon William Wyndham. He had served in the Coldstream Guards, but left in 1784 to marry Frances Mary Harford, the natural daughter of the last Lord Baltimore, after her marriage to a Mr Morris had been annulled. They spent much of their time abroad, but she was never happy and 'took up' with another lord – not a very happy background for the little boy who eventually became the last earl. It was recorded that in

The 4th Earl of Egremont as a midshipman

1799, when he was only 13, he joined the navy. This was still the navy of Lord Nelson, the navy of wood and sail and of great battles yet to come.

Family records give the impression of cousins on good terms with each other, of meetings between them in far flung corners of the globe, of snatched encounters on battlefields, and of a naval career that prospered with the help of his uncle, the third earl. Given that the family were all on good terms, the fourth earl's passion for building would seem to be just that. Most men of his era on attaining rank and wealth, sought to consolidate their position by acquiring a suitable estate with a suitable house. Henry Hoare at Stourhead is an early example; the Rothschilds at Mentmore and Waddesdon, and the Barings at Membland, are later ones. The third earl was 52 when his wife moved out of Petworth; the possibility of divorce and a legiti-

Blackborough House

mate son and heir could not have been ruled out. When she died in 1822, 15 years before her husband, that possibility must have been even stronger.

If outlandish was a fair description of Silverton Park, his lordship's principal residence, at least it had style, and a recognised architect. The same could not be said of his other excursions into the world of architecture, which included three large rectories.

All these pale into insignificance beside Blackborough House. High up on the Blackdown Hills in a commanding position there still stands this monument to the earl's taste in the extraordinary. A towering square of Victorian heaviness, unwelcoming in decay, it could never have been anything other than overbearing. It is in effect two houses, built back to back and separated by a courtyard. One half was for occupation by the rector of the newly completed Blackborough church, and the other was for the earl. It seems that Blackborough was designed and started before plans for Silverton were conceived. The estate and living had been in the Wyndham family for many generations and it may be that the earl was planning to reside chiefly on his estates at Orchard Wyndham, in Somerset. Plans had been drawn up for a very large residence – on a hilltop site without water – to supercede the ancient manorhouse of the Wyndhams. Fortunately, for whatever reason, this plan was abandoned.

Having made a choice in favour of Devon, it would naturally be unthinkable that an earl's principal residence should be of equal size and design and back to back with his rector – and so it would seem that the estate at Silverton became the prime objective. The choice was altogether more practical than the remote Blackdowns, reached only by a network of steep and twisting lanes – and with no near neighbours of suitable standing. Silverton was served by passable roads, close to Exeter and the neighbouring estates of Killerton, Poltimore, Newton St Cyres etc. It was also relatively close to the port of Topsham and his lordship, an ex-naval man, had a fully staffed yacht of which he made good use when it came to transporting weighty Italian marble statues, vases etc. for the adornment of his new house. It was also a useful disembarkation point for the building materials, though this consideration may not have been so important to the earl as the first!

Silverton occupies the site of a much older house, Combesatchfield, and it still seems somewhat strange that after all his grandiose plans, Lord Egremont should settle on rebuilding around an existing

Combesatchfield House

house. Perhaps by this time he was in a hurry to have something to show to the world, somewhere grand enough to go with his new position. But at least this decision does explain the unpretentious site of Silverton Park, down in the bottom of a dip, close to the public highway.

A Henry Langford of Dublin had bought Combesatchfield and it was the only property in the parish not owned by the Wyndhams; in 1720 Sir Henry Langford left the property to Thomas Brown who seems to have added his benefactor's name to his own.

The picture of Combesatchfield in Lord Coleridge's *Story of a Devonshire House* shows it to have been a pleasant mansion of the period about 1700 and Lord Coleridge gives an attractive picture of the serene and happy life spent there by the last of the Langford Browns to hold Combesatchfield – Mrs Dorothy Ayre Brown.

The great joy of all the boys was to spend their holidays with 'Aunt Brown' at Combesatchfield. Mrs Brown, the sister of Mrs James Coleridge, was the widow of Henry Langford Brown. Childless herself, she willingly adopted her nephews and neice. After the fashion of the day the two sisters called each other 'Mrs Brown' and 'Mrs Coleridge' and at the beginning of each holiday the same formula was used. 'Very well, Mrs Coleridge, I am very glad to have the boys, only remember I cannot answer for them and if they are drowned – and the ponds are very deep – or shoot themselves, or break their legs, I am not to blame'. This protest was, perhaps, not unnecessary when we know that there were two of these ponds on which excursions in tubs were wont to be made, also an old pistol or two, of which the boys had full command and horses with which they did pretty much as they liked.

Orchards too, gardens, fruit at discretion, a famous myrtle walk made Combesatchfield a paradise for the young. The mistress of the old fashioned stately square-built house was in keeping with its character. Too far from the Parish Church for her to walk, she always drove on Sunday in her dark green carriage with two fat horses and a postillion in drab jacket, a velvet cap surrounding all, with gold lace on the top. A very vision of splendour to youthful eyes. Every servant was to go to Church and the house, solitary as it was, to be locked up. She would not relax this rule, although every year on the Sunday before Silverton Fair, the garden, famous for its apricots was regularly robbed during Church time.

At Mrs Brown's death the property was sold in 1831 to Lord Egremont. He did not bother to pull down the old house but built a larger one round it in the then fashionable classic style; he renamed it Silverton Park.

He sent for workmen from Italy and kept them for many months casting the beautiful frieze which went all round the house and seemed to portray a long procession of people sacrificing bulls and colonnades of Corinthian pillars. There were 187 rooms with 150 cellars underneath the building, the whole occupying an acre of ground. It contained 130 marble mantlepieces and between 400 and 500 tablets formed the frieze round the house. In the centre of the south front was a stupendous high-relief of the nine Gods with Jupiter and his eagle in their midst. Inside the house the numerous bedrooms were no larger than a cabin in a Man of War, 'quite big enough for a batchelor' said Lord Egremont who had been a sailor. Each contained a bed and a tiny chest of drawers made to fit the rooms. One had no window but was lit by a skylight in the middle of the ceiling resembling an umbrella. His own bedroom was magnificent and his bath of yellow marble remained a wonder after all else had gone. The house is said to have cost almost a quarter of a million pounds – a stupendous sum in those days.

A generation later … he entered through the portico and after walking down a long passage came to the old green front door with its brass handle … And finally in 1900 the materials were

James Knowles' drawing for the interior of the hall at Silverton. There is no evidence as to whether this was ever executed
(British Architectural Library, RIBA)

sold to the housebreakers who blew it up with dynamite. The Italian additions were easily demolished, but the kernel, the old brick house, was of tougher mould and much of it still stands, a ruin which the kindly hand of time will soon make venerable. The ponds, except one gloomy excavation in the rock from which a spring wells forth, the park, the myrtle walk, all gone. (The Story of a Devonshire House, Lord Coleridge MCMVI)

This account makes plain that the inside of this fantastic pillared mansion was the plain brickbuilt 18th century house But it does seem incredible that after all his vast expenditure, the earl should have retained, unchanged, the original front door!

The Wyndham family still possesses the original accounts for the building of Silverton, and from these meticulously detailed invoices, a picture of the mansion emerges. The beautiful handwriting goes into the greatest detail, down to the last half inch and the last half penny. They put to shame the bald,

Account

computerised accounts of today – no future historian will have such luck as to uncover similar documents that provide not only a complete record but also a small piece of social history in that the rates paid to the labourers and craftsmen are also faithfully recorded.

The bulk of the work had been completed by the end of 1840 when W H J Hooper presented his bill to "The Right Honourable the Earl of Egremont for Work done at the Mansion, Silverton Park, Devonshire." The Hoopers seem to have been the main contractor, presenting in turn masons', carpenters', joiners', plumbers' accounts. An abstract of accounts at the end of the fat bundle summarises the totals involved. It seems his Lordship was indebted to the Hoopers to the tune of £67,838 10s 7½d, an enormous sum of money in those days. Although the accounts also include items for work done at

Orchard Wyndham and Blackborough House, the bulk of it was for Silverton Park.

The quantities given in these accounts give some indication of the sheer size of the undertaking:

1125 foot run of round brick columns built in roman cement with hard bricks carted from Exeter: cost £182 16s 3d.

The york lintels are listed in footage – 117ft of 8 inch, 504ft of 7 inch, 888ft of 6 inch, 76ft of 5 inch and 772 foot of 4 inch.

The mason's work totalled £22,093 19s 3d, plus another £958 for paving and bases of columns.

There was an ice house somewhere, for one item lists the perforating to the floor of the ice house.

The dairy shelves were of black and veined Devonshire marble slate with polished top and edges – 64 feet of it.

130 cubic yards of washed river sand and 2,570 bushells of Blackborough sand, washed and carried (£117 15s 10d) – this must have come fron quarries close to the Wyndham property at Blackborough.

7 Bundells of fir laths, 2 Bushells of Hair and 1200 lath nails came to 18s 2d – as there is a later item in the plasterer's account, this was probably for external work.

Then comes an item for metallic cement, an innovation that had obviously taken the earl's eye (he had it used at his previous home) because the entire house and stable block were covered in it – and it didn't come cheap. Perhaps it was supposed to be maintenance free; we shall never know as it only had to last for 50 years. 209 tons of it cost £418, and this was only a fraction of the total bill. This included the freight, expense of landing, and carriage to Silverton. Presumably it was shipped to Topsham, as this port seems to have been used for other goods by the earl.

River sand was used instead of common mortar, and 679 hogsheads of Blue lias lime instead of common lime (5s per hogshead extra), and totalling £169 15s.

12000 yards of digging and wheeling came to £300 and 267 door and window frames bedded, £13 7s. This account totalled £17,000 19s 9d.

The largest single item on the carpenter's account was for the oak lintels and floor joists, and fir ceiling joists. His total came to £7,092 18s 1d.

A statistician could probably work out the exact number of windows at Silverton from the joiner's details; 564ft of 3in moulded sashes; Wainscot Base and Meeting Rails in deal cased frame, oak sunk cills hung with lines, weights and axle pullies – total £84 12s 9d.

231ft of plate glass for the above windows in 4 pairs cost £164 11s 9d, followed by 115ft of Best Crown Glass in 2 pairs (£11 1s).

References to the 'old house' came in the carpenter's account with an item for blocking up doorways, removing partitions and taking up and relaying boarding.

730ft wainscot sash frames for metal sashes (£82 2s 6d); 200ft of 2$^{1/2}$inch moulded sashes framed, glazed and hung (£35 2s 11d); 3,169ft of 2 inch dittos (£518 3s 4d) and 7ft of 1$^{1/2}$ inch ditto (£1 2s 6d).

There were 714ft blank sashes and frames glazed, 50ft of 2$^{1/2}$ inch moulded sashes glazed and fixed, and 71ft of 2 inch ditto.

There is reference to a Sculpture room and Butler's Pantry, then an item for 235ft deal cased frames. The floors were of 1$^{1/2}$ inch best yellow deal dowelled.

Then came the doors. 253ft of 3 inch double moulded 4 panel doors (£37 19s) with Artragal on the panels.

This is followed by 420ft of 2$^{1/2}$ inch ditto, 609ft of 2 inch ditto and 676ft of 2$^{1/2}$ inch bead flush both side solid 4 panel doors.

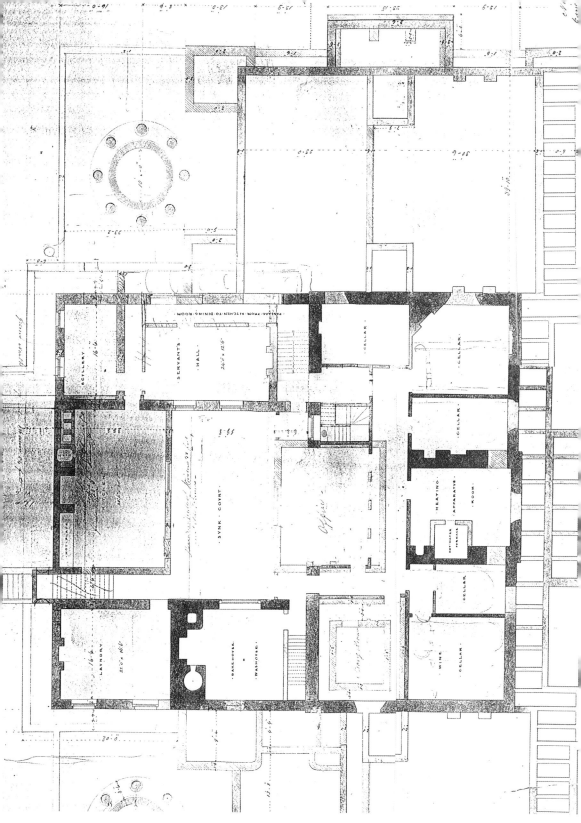

Basement plans from James Knowles' unfinished drawings for Silverton Park

On a more intimate scale, there is an item for 11 Spanish mahogany framed seats, risers, skirtings all complete fixed to Waterclosets on bearers (£46 4s) and two deal waterclosets (£3 10s).

The butler had a bedstead in his closet – not only did it save his mixing with the lower orders of male servants, but meant he could keep an eye on the family plate – and the wine cellar! Way down on the list is flywire in the Larder and Dairy doors and to the wine cellar, and superfine Crimson cloth for doors (£32 9s).

In all the joiner's account came to £4,486.

Reading through these accounts opens the windows on to another world, a completely different way of life, and makes a generation used to everything mechanical sit and think just how such huge building projects were undertaken, and so successfully completed. No concrete mixers, no JCB's, no delivery lorries with jib cranes, no handy DIY store down the road. Everything was brought to the site by horse and cart, and in the case of the joiners and carpenters, made up there. It was a huge undertaking, and necessitated the creation of a 'brick field' which contained suitable clay which was dug, shaped and fired on site. This made bricks a costly item and they were only used when there was no nearby quarry or other source of stone rubble.

In 1838 there is an entry 'Delivered to the brick field, 829 doz of furze – £497 8s, at 12s per doz.

The brickmaker must have died some time that year as there is a letter to the earl dated 4th December 1838,

Sir, The widdow of the late James Phillips Deceased would feel Particularly obliged if you could name a day for the Settlement of the Brick Account As She is in want of cash,
    Yours Respectfully on behalf of the widdow
    W Phillips.

The amount was £588 13s and it is to be hoped the 'Widdow' was not kept waiting too long.

From the ironmonger's account some idea of the sumptuousness of the interior begins to emerge; ten sets of ivory furniture (for the doors) with ormulu Bands made in London to order cost £26 with 18 ivory shutter knobs to match, and 'superior' brass shutter latches with ivory furniture. Even the stables had brass door furniture. Plates, hinges, chains, locks etc came to £412 5s 1d.

The painter's account is interesting – everything was well and truly painted with, in some cases, five coats of oil based paint. He covered 2,585½ yards with four coats in oil (£118 10s 0½d) and 35 yards, five times.

The skirtings are itemised – covered 4 times – 2,275ft of 15 inch skirting, 420ft of 12 inch, 299ft of 9 inch and 298ft of 7 inch. 139½ doz sash squares were painted five times (outside) 156 frames, and 124 doz squares – only four times (inside) and 13 chimney pieces. The only mention of colour is green, but there is a further painter's account dealing with the wall finishes.

A further 95 sash frames and 14 chimney pieces are accounted for – perhaps in the staff quarters – and the total was £552 14s 6d.

The plumber supplied 14 patent waterclosets with Basons and apparatus for £126. His total came to £5,689 17s 8d and included over 5 tons of sheet lead at £200, a 1,184ft run of 6 inch lead rainwater pipe, 63ft 9 inch of 5 inch and 29ft 6 inch of 4 inch, plus 1,116ft run of 1½ inch stout drawn pipe.

The plasterer covered 4,436 yards with lath and plaster – £554 10s, and 2,340 yards of render. His account itemises roman cement, render – stucco plain face, 1,437 yards lime whited to coats, enriched mouldings and cement skirting, 'Grecian frets', pateras and papier mache flowers and fixing, cost £1,855

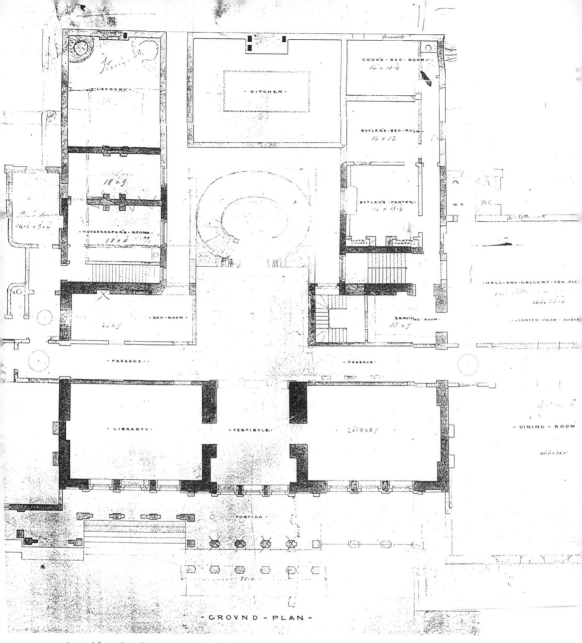

Ground floor plans from James Knowles' unfinished drawings for Silverton Park

3s 11d, and his total bill was £2,277 12s 6d.

The smith's account includes work done to the stable buildings and the first item is for a 141ton 13cwt cast iron Girder including Carriage Hoisting at £16 per ton – £2,266 8s. It also includes cast iron brackets and shoes for the billiard room (£27 9s) and labour and patterns for the brackets. This item highlights the way craftsmen worked and were able to make up their own moulds and patterns on site. The smith was also responsible for 12 cwt of wrought iron balustrades and newels to the stone staircase (£27 10s 10d) and two large cast iron moulded newels, a 99ft run of handrail and 156 holes cut in the stone steps for the iron baluster. A further item is for two cast iron doors to the strong closet (12cwt).

The painter's bill does not tell us if his bill relates to any specific rooms in the mansion; presumably

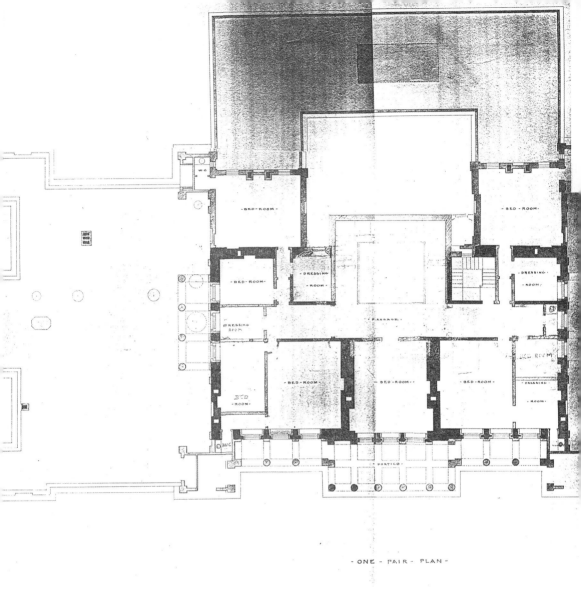

First floor plans from James Knowles' unfinished drawings for Silverton Park

he is giving the details of the principal rooms in detailing the finishes: the distemper was blue and the oil paint, cream. The enriched bead was picked out with gold, and 'Husk ornament Gilt solid flatted and distemper', Grecian scroll ornament, Honeysuckle ornament and one large centre flower and one small ditto, with 30 Grecian Pateras. This must have been a very magnificent room! Having finished his gilding, he then turned his attention to the woodwork and treated 250 yards 'grained in imitation of Birds Eye Maple and varnished three times, plus 'skirting as above' – was it panelling, or wainscotting or the doors that were so painted? – or perhaps the shutters to the windows? In addition there were 786 yards painted once in oil in imitation of wainscot and twice varnished, four large sash windows painted in oil (five times) grained maple and 55 sash frames similarly treated.

The varnish employed for the above, we are told, was supplied by the earl. One wonders why.

It was not only the actual building that had to be accounted for. In an era when road travel was still the exception rather than the norm, and roads poorly, if at all surfaced, the logistics of transporting the

105

vast quantity of materials for such a large project must have been a considerable headache. There is an item for three carts and two horses, for drawing iron cisterns, for stables, dog kennels and gardens, for marble paving for the bathrooms, skirting, chimney pieces, slate, salting, cisterns, stoves, pump and ironmongery from Exeter – cost £1 10s. This was followed by another illuminating entry – two waggons and three horses were paid 18s for drawing empty cases back to Topsham. The accounts tell us that a man, cart and horse for six days received £1 16s per day whilst working on the estate. The earl's large marble bath took four horses a day to draw it up from Exeter. Also brought up was a load of water closets and old marble fireplaces – it would seem there is nothing new about architectural salvage.

The account for the metallic sand was kept in its entirety, although there are no details of its composition. The suppliers were Messrs. Wm E Logan and Charles Dyer of 4, New Broad Street, London and their total bill amounted to £3,201 8s 10$^{1/2}$d. A separate account appears for interest charged on the outstanding balance of £2,000, finally settled on 4th December, 1841.

Listed are four ionic capitals to columns and fixings; 24 ditto; 24$^{1/2}$ ditto; 96 lions heads, 102 headings and bottoms of flutes and columns, and 580 Dentils. Metallic cement castings prepared but not fixed: 4 Ionic capitals to columns, 32 Corinthian ditto, 457 dentils for upper entablature, 120 Modillions, 142 small trusses, 162 pateros and 20 lions masks.

The same firm carried out further work in 1842 (£1,128) and 1843 (£1,622 19 6$^{3/4}$d).

Apparently applying metallic cement must have been a messy business for there is an item for cleaning 110 squares of glass in the kitchen, housekeepers room and bedrooms in the 'old house', and for glass broken by the metallic plasters, £2 7s 6d.

There were ashlar stone jambs to the entrance to the dung pit, and these, together with the pebble paving to the stables, cost £3,001 17s 2d. The external stone walling cost £1,253 14s, and the total for the gardens etc. came to a further £2,752 11s 6d.

And it was all approved by James Knowles, the architect.

An Abstract of Daywork at the gardens from 8th September to 22nd December, 1839, tells us that the carpenter spent 312 days 8 hrs, wages £62 11s 4d; the bricklayer spent 50 days and his labourer 28 days, and they used 3,606 bricks and 125 fine bricks, and with six days put in by the plumber, the total came to £3,050 13s. The daily rate for the carpenter and bricklayer was 4 shillings, and 2s 4d for their labourer.

A separate account concerns the building of the Viaduct and Park Walls, and starts with an item for three men spending seven days in felling trees and taking down hedges, excavating and wheeling. This is a reference to the realignment of the parish road which had formerly passed in front of the house, but was now to run on an embankment, and then through a cutting behind the house – as it still does. The stone walling also still stands; 2945 perches of it cost £1,767, and the elliptical brick arch through which the drive passes was a further £64 9s. The park doors were painted in Brunswick Green and the total bill for the viaduct and walling came to £2,108 7s 6d.

Way down the account is an item for 37$^{1/4}$lbs of candles at 8d, and to rubbish baskets for £1 5s.

And it cost his lordship 18 shillings for engraving 12 keys with a number, Silverton Park, and the coronet. Did any of them survive?

The whole place must have buzzed with activity. A constant stream of traffic would have clogged up the lanes, and probably reduced the surfaces to a muddy quagmire. The locals must have been agog and those who were not directly employed probably walked over to see the progress on his lordship's mansion. For many of them it must have brought welcome employment, and the hope of a future linked to the great house, either as servants or suppliers of labour and provisions.

Did they all marvel at the sums of money spent and the size and quality of the building they were helping to erect, proud of their own small part – or were they aghast at the extravagance?

Whilst work was going on at the mansion, and in fact before it had even begun in earnest, the earl was spending on improving the grounds. The accounts that have survived are largely from the old-established nursery of Veitch & Son, then operating at Mount Radford and Killerton, outside Exeter. This nursery was active in plant hunting expeditions, and in the propagation and hybridisation of many fine species and it is probable that the earl benefitted from this. Reading down the long and detailed lists of plants supplied, the gardens and grounds of Silverton Park must have been beautiful indeed, and had the house survived then the garden would surely have become one of Devon's premier attractions.

The earliest account is for trees supplied in 1837/8 and included 5,020 large trees for the plantations and the hill above the new road – £150 15s. The varieties planted elsewhere in the grounds included oak, elm, Spanish and horse chestnut, birch, Turkey oak, lime, beech, sycamore, Scottish laburnum, mountain ash, robinia, bignonia, walnuts and acacias. Later accounts list red cedars, and over the next few years well over 1,000 large laurels and a similar number of small laurels were supplied as well as hollies, privet, and almost every kind of shrub then known to the horticultural world. Amongst the ornamental varieties were 30 large rhododendrons, 100 small ditto, numerous azaleas listed by colour but not variety, lilacs, guelder roses, honeysuckles, roses, buddleas and so on, The 1840 account totals £256 2s 6d.

Probably to adorn his greatly enhanced gardens, the earl had shipped from Genoa four marble vases and the bill survives from 1843 recording their shipping from London to Topsham in November, referring to their great weight and bulk and the fact that the vases had arrived unharmed: cost of shipping £25 16s.

The bill for seeds and plants supplied for the kitchen gardens list many varieties now long fallen by the wayside – Blue peas, black and white radish and also grown for the earl's table were cardoon, salsify, cherville, angelica, sweet Basil, savory, Batavian endive, Kohl Rabi, Borecol, Danish Brocoli. These were enlivened with 200 hollyhocks, dahlias, lilies, gladioli, lupins, yellow ranunculus, delphinium, violets, anemones, pinks, double polyanthus, white rocket, hepatica, heartsease, stocks and gentians. (An account book for 1877 shows that produce was sold regularly at Covent Garden.)

The Exeter nursery of Luccome Pince & Co sent a bill dated 5 April, 1843 for supplying trees including 200 elms, oaks, flowering chestnuts and 100 standard apples – variety not stated, 30 very fine large horsechestnuts and six very fine weeping limes, 100 canadian poplars and 100 Lombardy poplars, 12 cedar of Lebanon and three magnolias.

They had barely time to settle down before the earl died in 1845.

This account of the impressive funeral of the 4th Earl comes from *The Devonshire Chronicle & Exeter News*, 15th April 1845.

On Wednesday the mournful and extensive cavalcade which conveyed the remains of the late Earl of Egremont to his last resting place set out from Silverton Park to Orchard Wyndham where the family vault is situate. The procession was escorted by the tenantry amounting to about 100 persons through Bradninch and Cullompton, the bells of the respective churches being tolled and continued along the route. On Thursday at Orchard Wyndham the procession was formed from the mansion of the late earl to the church. It was preceded by the tenantry in mourning and was headed by four mutes after whom plumes of feathers were carried. Then came the coronet of the late earl bourne by an esquire and escorted by pages. The bearers followed, after whom came the hearse containing the body of the deceased, placed in a mahogany shell enclosed in a state coffin covered with blue velvet and adorned with silver ornaments. The hearse was escorted by eight sailors comprising the yacht establishment of the late earl, their arms being encircled with crape. The whole procession was said to have extended for one mile. The solemnity of the scene was suggestive of many mournful thoughts in the minds of the spectators as the grave closed over the last of the lords of Egremont.

According to the same newspaper, his death was unexpected and it is stated that "a few days before his death his lordship made a Will, but in whose favour is not yet known."

At the time of his death he was involved in controversy over the leases of several properties in the Taunton and Somerset areas of the estate, granted by the 3rd Earl. Apparently his lordship was seeking to recover the properties without compensation on the grounds that the leases were invalid. There had been one law suit brought against him which had been upheld in court, and the issue of 5th April 1845 carried a vituperative letter from 'A lessee' damning the Earl of Egremont for his actions and the misery and suffering caused by his revocation of the Leases. The Editor notes that he had 'omitted certain passages as the earl is not in a fit state of mind to hear the whole truth at once.' He had in fact died three days previously.

Almost immediately some of the contents and possessions were sold off.

At Park Farm on the estate on 23rd and 24th April, 1845, there was a sale of the property of the late Earl of Egremont. 5 carriage horses fetched £65, £75 and £21; Cob horses, mare and harness £363 13s 6d.

6 donkeys fetched £1 7s each followed by ewes and hogs, goat, Guernsey cow, several cows – all named – bull, pigs – total £864.

The second day totalled £1,130 16s 5d and included carts, and gig; £11 for a water cart; cooper's implements from the brewery, geese, ducks, chickens and turkeys; a Macaw in its cage was sold for £2 10s; 28 doz of pigeons went to new homes, plus owls in a cage, guinea fowls, rabbits etc.

In 1845 there was a further sale at Topsham of all the nautical items but not the yacht itself, and in the same year, in August, Christie's in London sold the Countess's china and wine which seemed to go amazingly cheaply; £1 7s for a Worcester tea and coffee service; no price given for an Oriental tea and coffee service in blue and gold 39 pieces, many richly enamelled. A blue stone china dinner service of 18 dishes and 8 doz table plates made £9 and the Sevres dessert service in green, pair of ice pails, pair of baskets, pair of bowls and 24 plates, fetched 19 guineas. There was a service of French glass - 37 items. The sale ended with 2 large iron beams (£14) and 2 iron columns, a quantity of blue liass, saltes at the workshops (£10) materials of the workshops and stones worked for sinks (£15). In all a total of £132 19s 3d.

The wine did better, bringing in a total of £2,211 8s 5d.

Samples of wines may be had by paying for same on application to Mr Woods, the butler.

The wines all went for around £8 per doz. There were 17 doz old port, 48 lots of 3 doz port each, sherry, madeira, claret, champagne, burgundy.

Then came 185 lots including 4 lots of cyder, 3 doz of very old port, 2 doz from the Duke of Somerset's cellar, and a further 36 lots of 3 doz port, hock burgundy, chablis etc. 370 lots in all, and ended with 1 doz whiskey, from the Duke of Sussex cellar – £2 10s.

Christies had also auctioned the rare stove and greenhouse plants, in August, which ran to 1018 lots of acacias, camellias, yucca, gloxinia, gardenia, begonia, passiglor, orange tree in fruit (14s), fig trees (4s), 21 orange trees - total £104 18s.

From then until 1892 when the sale of the furniture took place, Silverton fades completely. The countess had died in 1876. There seem to be no records or memories of those twilight years, except one mention:

> The lovely vanished house … [was] built by my grandfather's half-brother, the last Earl of Egremont … As a small child I stayed there frequently, with his widow, my great-aunt … who out-lived her husband many years. I can remember … playing in and out of the colonnades as a child, and as a great treat the steward used to unlock the unfinished rooms for my nurse and myself to see … the floors were unboarded and chimneypieces unfinished, and there were large wooden cases, containing marbles and carvings, which Lord Egremont had brought from Italy and Florence in his yacht … My great-aunt used to drive in a yellow coach from Orchard Wyndham to Silverton and stay a few months in each place. (Country Life correspondence, 21 Sept 1945)

Perhaps it was used occasionally for holidays, perhaps it was shut up, ignored. There does not seem to have been any attempt made to sell or let the place. From the details of the contents sale, it would appear to have been left more or less as Lord Egremont left it.

The auction catalogue for the sale of 'Costly, Rare and Valuable Antique Furniture' makes interesting reading. It lists 60 Bed, Dressing and Reception rooms, not the 187 rooms mentioned in the Coleridge account. Even so, the sale was held over three days, 6th, 7th and 8th December, 1892, and refreshments were available on each day, the sale commencing at 11.30 a.m. to enable buyers to reach Silverton via rail from London, Bath, Bristol, Torquay or Taunton. The East Wing bedrooms came first with the usual birch bedstead, feather bed, bolster and 2 pillows, mahogany washstand with "5 pieces of ware and footbath", carpet and curtains to each room. No 7 and 8 bedrooms were grander, with a carved mahogany 4-post bedstead (2 guineas) a carved mahogany easy chair (4 guineas), a sponge bath and, in bold type, a "very fine Walnut Cabinet, fitted with drawers and heavily brass mounted, 5ft 8in high by 3ft 2in" – sold for £20.

The gallery was used for display and items offered were "8 Egyptian figures, 4 silver Buddhas, 2 Egyptian figures in basalt, model of a cutter yacht with carved figurehead, 7 stalactite carvings, bag of 28 old Roman bronze coins, contents of 3 undershelves – shells fossils etc.", and a 10ft mahogany Chippendale bookcase.

There was also 36ft of staircarpet to the ground floor, 19 brass stair rods and 21 ditto. Unfortunately, no prices are given here.

Lord Egremont was evidently a great collector of books, as well as souvenirs brought home from his travels. The list of books in the library runs to five pages, lots 217-363, catalogued in some detail, and presumably the star attraction of the sale. Many of them dated from the early 1700's, and some were from the Continent. The highest price went to 172 volumes bound in calf of the Gentleman's Magazine 1731-1842 – £17 0s.

All these had been housed on two runs of 36ft of shelving in two recesses, and an 8ft 8in bookcase. The library also contained various items of porcelain, and a French mahogany and satinwood secretaire with marble top, and a walnut inlaid writing table with ormolu mountings.

LOT

489 Handsome carved and gilt and white side table with grey marble top, 4ft.9in.

490 A marble bust

1 Upright clock in walnut case, with brass face .. 6 gns

2 Case barometer

3 A beautifully inlaid LOUIS XIV. CABINET, brass-mounted with marble top, 3 ft. by 3 ft. .. 10 gns

4 A ditto 3 ft. 9 in. .. 16-10

5 A ditto 3 ft. 9 in. .. 8-10

6 A marble bust (female) .. 3 gns

7 "Chinese Mandarin," carved wood and heavily gilt, 28 in. .. 5-15

8 A ditto ditto .. 7 gns

9 Carved wood figure of Chinese lady, 20 in. high .. 2-8

500 Pair granite Corinthian pedestals 4 ft. high .. 8

1 Pair ditto ditto

2 Bronzed draped bust on marble stand .. 7-15

3 Marble bust .. 3-6

4 Marble head and 2 specimens polished jasper .. 2-16

5 Fender and fire irons

6 Plaster cast of 2 females (draped)

7 Draped figure of female

8 Ditto

9 19 in. Chinese bronze bason decorated with lizards and elephants heads to the feet (a very fine specimen) .. 5 gns

510 7 in. bronze bason (very old) and 2 old pewter jugs and covers

1 Five marble statuettes (damaged) .. 2-15

2 Inlaid cedar cabinet .. 1-10

3 Mahogany cabinet and contents (fossils, &c.) .. 1-10

4 Handsome inlaid and ormolu mounted LOUIS XIV. WRITING TABLE 6ft. 4 in. by 3 ft. with 3 drawers .. 22

5 EGYPTIAN MUMMY in case in excellent preservation .. 13-10

6 A ditto ditto .. 9

7 Two marble mortars

8 An old carved oak panel from Perranzabuloe .. 2 gns

9 Two Buhl wall brackets .. 3 gns

520 A marble column 4 ft. 6 in. .. £2

1 Half circular CHIPPENDALE CONSOLE TABLE with medallions .. 25

2 A ditto to match

3 Pair blue Japanese vases, 24 in. .. 4-8

4 Plaster bust

5 A ditto

6 Carved oak OCTAGON TABLE, 3 ft. 8 in. .. 6-10

7 Oval oak table, 6 ft. 6 in. by 3 ft. 4 in. .. 2-17-6

8 Bronze ewer on stand with cover .. 6

9

The second day commenced with bedrooms in the west wing. The Earl of Egremont's bedchamber contained a "famous old maple and gilt 4-post Canopy Bedstead with blue tabaret furniture and surmounted by cornice and gilt coronet (£8) and a hair mattress (very large, 2 guineas)," and four sets of birds eye maple drawers and cupboards with circular ends. In the boudoir were 2 dragon ornaments, a mahogany writing case, telescope and 2 hassocks.

Then followed 13 Etruscan vases, several items of patera, and Roman and Greek vases etc.

The dining room had the usual stuffed birds and animals, sideboards etc. several small tables and "set of Massive Spanish Mahogany Dining Tables with spare leaves and mahogany stand extending to 32ft by 4ft 9in wide" (£26 10s).

The contents of the drawing room and the large dining room are interesting. Instead of the expected fine collection of furniture and ornaments, both rooms were full of bedroom items; 9 bedsteads in the drawing room and 23 in the large dining room, with washstands, chests of drawers, mattresses etc. The carpet in the large dining room was 26ft by 12ft, and also offered were two runs of bordered staircarpet, 50 feet each.

Three large cases containing plaster for a handsome centrepiece suitable for a drawing room or a large public hall (unpacked) was the first lot offered in the Billiard Room. Later lots were for fragments of marble, statuettes, stone carvings and all kinds of oddments including several lots of white polished marble slabs, 3ft by 1ft 6in. For 70 guineas someone bought the "Valuable marble relief 'Virgin Mary and Child' by Carew, 3ft 10in x 3ft 5in, originally said to have cost 300 guineas, a beautiful chef d'oeuvre suitable for a church." Another seeming bargain was the noble "Italian white marble mantel 8ft wide by 3ft 4in by 3ft, originally costing 500 guineas" – and sold for 170 guineas.

All these beautiful items must still exist – do their owners know that they once graced the ornate home of the last Earl of Egremont?

After all the finery and foreign marble, ending with two magnificently carved Caen Stone Pedestals and Bases, it must have been something of an anti-climax to descend to the basement and the servants' quarters. In the Servants' Hall was a 29ft run of 28in oak benching on 10 iron brackets, a deal table, and not much else. The brewery, indispensable in any large establishment, was intact with its four copper vats and sundry equipment. The butler's pantry still contained the birch folding bed and cupboard mentioned in the builder's accounts, and the servants' sitting room was equipped with cocoa matting, five chairs, a mahogany card table and a spanish table, 10ft 3in by 4ft. The kitchen must have been depleted earlier as only minimal contents were listed. Nowhere is there any china or plate, or glassware of any kind. The stables and outbuildings are not mentioned at all.

Not included in the sale, but listed in an inventory are some of the better furnishings and paintings.

Drawing room – 2 sofas, easy chairs, leather-covered reclining chair, American rocking chair, screens, tables.

Library – beautiful old Buhl table with masks in ormulu, the top covered with leather (this is the in drawing room in the sale catalogue), *Brussels carpets, crimson cloth curtains, in dining room.*

Earl of Egremont's bedroom – blue tarbret bed hangings and gilt coronet

The pictures listed include Gainsborough in the hall, and a Poussin, Romney, many Italian works including Tintoretto's *Judith and Holofernes*; in the library were Poussin, Sir Joshua Reynolds' *Laughing Girl*; another Reynolds in the drawing room, and a Van Dyck self portrait; Reubens, Gainsborough, and Van Dyke's *Christ Betrayed*. There were also Reynolds, Reubens' *Portrait of Marquis of Granby* in the dining room; Van Eyke in the passage, and Tintoretta in the study; Gainsborough and Kneller in the dressing room with some Hogarths. In all around 200 works of art were listed.

East wing servants rooms are referred to as the Old House, and no room was specially apportioned to the Countess.

The final end of Silverton is not well documented. It was demolished 'around 1900' by a builder from Cullompton. He did a very thorough job, though no doubt there are bits and pieces of the old house to be found in many of the nearby farms and cottages, and in the present Combesatchfield house.

In 1915, the site, park and 2,000 acres and the stable block were sold.

For many years the stables were used as farmbuildings, and occupied as a farmhouse. Then in 1987 Mr B G Hawkins, of The Park, Silverton, offered them for sale, having built himself a new farmhouse. The purchaser was The Landmark Trust, who proposed to renovate this remarkable range of buildings, and using their team of experts, to recreate the stables as they would have appeared when Lord Egremont's carriage with its four horses which he habitually drove, clattered over the cobbled yard. Inside they will create a comfortable holiday home, enjoying pleasant views over the quiet Devon countryside.

Will the Landmark Trust, I wonder, recoat it all in that famous bronze metallic cement?

When the Wyndham family sold off the Kentisbeare and Blackborough estates in 1915, Blackborough house was described:

It was erected at a cost of £32,000, and contained a total of 34 bed and dressing rooms, 2 bathrooms with marble baths, 6 entertaining rooms etc...

The property having been unoccupied has been allowed to get into a state of disrepair, but could easily be restored and converted into a hospital, sanatorium or convalescent home. 'The

The stable block

property will be sold at such a price that it will be a profitable purchase for contractors, builders, plumbers and speculators to pull down the edifice and release the VALUABLE MATERIALS which include many tons of lead roofing, flashing parapet, rain water pipes, thousands of good quality slates, 25 beautiful red, blue, grey and white marble mantelpieces, 2 marble baths, several solid 8-panelled mahogany doors on rising brass butt-hinges, numerous mahogany sideboard and recess fitting, doors floorboards etc.

It was sold to Mr Hughes for £1050 and was 'stripped of everything' although it was later taken over by the Council, re-roofed and made habitable and used for training purposes.

A sale of furniture purchased new by the late Earl of Egremont had been held on the premises on 2nd June 1845. It included dinner, dessert, breakfast and tea services, rich cut glass, marble bath, Brussels carpets etc.

Only the best bedroom had a carved 4-poster; there were yards of stair and passage carpets; mahogany chest of drawers, washstands, bedsteads, etc.

Bedrooms 5-9 were reached by the upper staircase.

The wine cellar contained 2 doz 15 year old port, various other lots of madeira, champagne, etc, and one empty bottle!

The drawing room was 'finely furnished' with satinwood card tables, 8-day clock, vases, etc.

The dining room had a 13ft by 5ft Spanish mahogany table.

Lot 241 was a handsome purple and gold dinner service of 112 pieces (£4 8s) and figured china service of 71 pieces (£1 8s).

Bedrooms 10, 11 and 12 and 13 were on the second day with the servants hall, butlers pantry and kitchen.

The wine and china sale totalled £171 4s 6d and included 13 ton 16 cwt of coal sold for £13 11s.

The total sale fetched £587 10s 10d.

Blackborough was again auctioned on 26 October 1923. The details were very briefly given on one sheet of foolscap paper, but it stated that the house was in a partial state of demolition and partial reconstruction and there was a large quantity of material on site to assist in putting the mansion in a sound state of repair.

It has not been occupied for a very long period and during the War was partly demolished. Nearly all the beautiful marble mantelpieces are still intact needing only to be replaced in their original positions together with several solid panelled mahogany, Austrian oak and deal and pitch pine doors.

Splendid entrance hall 35ft by 8ft by 14ft with central heating stove, cloak room and lavatory; No 1 reception room 20ft 6in by 19ft by 14ft, Bay 11ft by 4ft, stone floor, fireplace; No 2 reception room, 17ft by 15ft by 14ft, fireplace, splendid views; 2 small reception rooms. Bathroom; servants pantry; WC; kitchen 14ft 6in by 12ft by 14ft, good range and boiler.

On the east side, walled in space 52ft 6in by 20ft with large windows would make a splendid billiard room if glass roof thrown over. Larder; large cellar.

Splendid bold spiral staircase leading to first floor; landing 34ft 6in by 11ft 6in with dresser. Excellent bedrooms and convenient corridors; bedroom 1 16ft 3in by 11ft 6in, bedroom 2 20ft by 18ft 6 in; bedrooms 6, 7 and 8 are on the second floor.'

Blackborough House, 1913

Lot 2 was accommodation land and a building site.

Today half is a ruin, and half occupied by a firm of carbreakers.

Blackborough church, too, has been demolished. It was found to be structurally unsound, and too remote and costly to repair, so yet another of the earl's proud new buildings has come to an early end.

The old house in decay. The windows are boarded up, the ivy begins to take a hold, but the mullion windows and front door have not been removed. Note the obvious roofline to the original house

Fowlescombe

THE tale of Fowlescombe is nearly told. Ivy has all but won its battle, and before many more winters have passed, all will be over. What little remains of the outer walls serves only as a climbing frame for the dense swags and curtains of glossy green foliage, the thick trunks embedded in the masonry. The inner walls are laid bare with all pretence of it ever having been a habitation gone for ever.

All around lies the debris of a ruined house. Fallen stonework, some dressed, some shaped from doors and windows, most just piles of rubble. No trace of timbers, or lath and plaster, remain. No windows, no glass, no doors, no hearthstones, no roofs or ceilings. Nothing.

But Fowlescombe was once a beautiful house, beautifully situated. To say it 'nestles' in its valley for once is a true description. Well hidden from prying eyes, it lies about halfway down a long winding combe, tucked in under the sheltering lee of the hill. It faces south, and when the old stonework was bathed in the warmth of the suns rays, the mullioned windows reflecting back the evening glow, Fowlescombe must have been a lovely sight. The approach is down a long drive where the remnants of an avenue of lime and plane trees proclaim that this was once the way to a house of quality.

Today, the visitor – or trespasser for visitors are not welcome – first passes the deserted lodge at Fowlescombe Cross. This would appear to be of relatively modern construction, and the sweep of the walls and the imposing gate pillars, once surmounted by large granite finials, were carried out in some style.

The lodge is derelict. The granite orbs have long since fallen. If there were ever ornamental gates, these too have gone and in their place an old farm gate is tied up with twine, discouraging all but the most determined of visitors. The track descends gently under the trees, and there is nothing to be seen but fields on either side. About a quarter of a mile down, two smaller granite posts look as if they once had some purpose, perhaps to mark the end of the farmlands and the beginning of the parkland.

The drive continues. Past a gently decaying caravan. Then a farmhouse and its outbuildings come into view. The farmhouse looks pleasant enough, but nothing exceptional; surely the outbuildings are more substantial and more numerous than is normal? And beyond the entrance to the farm are another pair of granite pillars, this time with smaller granite balls still in situ, giving entrance to the farmyard. The drive continues downwards, curving gently around the valley side. A widening stream runs down through the lush green meadows and as the valley opens out some interesting walls on the far side proclaim that the search is nearly over. These are the remains of the stables, however, and must have been approached via the farmyard higher up, as there is no way across the meadows at this point. The walls are still fairly intact, but the yard is a quagmire, effectively deterring exploration.

As the eye becomes accustomed to seeking out fragments of walls, it becomes apparent that the trees of ivy lower down the valley conceal all that is left of Fowlescombe.

It is something of a shock.

1997, from across the causeway

From the house a drive crossed the meadows; though it is many long years since carriage wheels passed this way, the line of the causeway on which the drive was raised is still plain. As it approached the main drive it was carried on an embankment across the stream. Two large ponds lie below, and another pair of granite pillars mark the point where it joins the main drive.

At some stage the whole valley seems to have been cultivated. The stream is dammed in several places and lower down there is evidence of further ponds, and what appears to be the remains of terracing.

Fowlescombe, according to Professor Hoskin, was built in 1537 by Sir Thomas Fowlescombe. His house was modest in size and unpretentious in design. It grew over the centuries – and at some time between 1792 and 1865 was greatly enlarged with the main front being almost doubled in length.

1997, the west front

From the evidence on the ground it is difficult to envisage the interior. All is now a shambles with mounds of debris, nettles and brambles. The house was built almost into the rock and a narrow passageway runs between the hewn rockface and the rear wall against which were a number of small rooms or outhouses, perhaps fronting onto an internal courtyard. In the centre there is the remains of what was obviously an outside staircase, but without a massive clearing operation it is difficult even to conjecture. The maze of walls that crisscross the inner area may have been underfloor supports rather than clues to room divisions, but it would seem that the house was only one room deep.

The west-facing front, more or less symmetrical from the outside, has strange angles inside, indicating alterations over the years. To make an entrance, part of a room was lost and there is evidence of former windows on what had been an outside wall. This then, was the first enlargement to the original house – a new front and entrance. The corner tower is of great antiquity and once had a small external

1997. The interior, looking towards the west entrance

door, long blocked up. A few clues come from the exposed wall surfaces and it is probable that Fowlescombe was originally a hall house extending from the corner tower, including the clock tower and the two bays beyond, but stopping short of the next tower. The main entrance would have been under the clock (though that was a later addition), opening on to a screens passage running to the rear. To the left would have been the great hall with its lovely mullioned window and huge fireplace.

Mr G Copeland visited Fowlescombe in March 1944 and found that "Time and weather have done little more to alter the general appearance of this sorry wreck of a mansion. More plaster has fallen off the SW porch and revealed one original stone quoin." He then details what he found, in his own architectural shorthand – but it seems there was little left except for the granite lintels of two minor fireplaces. The 2-arched bridge across the artificial lake was becoming very overgrown, and he mentions the two long parallel walled gardens behind the house. The entrance lodge he describes as "semi-oct. pseudo-Tudor with semi-oct. gate-piers," and concludes "It seems clear that, apart from considerable extension in the early 19th century every attempt by means of sham Tudor work in stucco and plaster was made to obliterate the details of the 16th century house and perhaps most of its plan and elevation."

The Fowells rose to prominence as lawyers – a common link with many other family fortunes founded around this time.

William Fowell was MP for Totnes in 1455 and died in Ugborough parish in 1507. He is described as 'of Fowellscombe' as are the three preceding generations. (Vivians Visitations of Devon, 1895). They must have had a dwelling somewhere, but whether it was on the same site is not known.

Lysons (Magna Britannica 1822) tells us that "Fowellscombe belonged for many descents to the family of Fowell and the first on record was an attorney in the reign of Henry IV"; Sir Edmond was created a baron in 1661 and died in 1674, aged 81. He "enjoined his sons John and Edmond that if both should die without male issue then living, either of them who should be in possession of the Barton or farms of Fowelscombe, Boulterscombe and Witchcombe and the manor of Ludbrook, should leave them to this William Fowell. The last baronet, having no male issue, left all the estates to him and constituted him sole executor of his will."

This was Sir John, a grandson, who died on 26th November, 1692, aged only 27, leaving two sisters, Elizabeth and Margaret, married to Arthur Champernowne of Dartington. Lysons, again, states that "the estate was brought to the Champernownes, who sold it in 1758 to the father of George Herbert, esq, who sold it to Thomas King."

William Fowell, born in 1566, is the first recorded Fowell to live at Black Hall, whilst his elder brother, Arthur (father of Sir Edmond), continued at Fowelscombe. It was this William's grandson, another William, who stood to inherit both estates should the senior male line fail.

It is not clear how the Champernownes managed to hold on to Fowelscombe; perhaps they bought it back from William, but Margaret is recorded as living there as a widow, dying in 1730, and leaving Fowelscombe to her third son Henry, who died in 1757.

Polwhele's *History of Devon*, written in 1796, gives a different view by stating that the two sisters were aunts of the last baronet, and were co-heiresses who split the estates. He ends by saying that "Herbert Esq., sold it to Mr Th. King, who is daily improving both the venerable mansion and its valuable appurtenances."

The King family came from Buckfastleigh and Dean Prior, outside Plymouth, where they had brewing interests with property in Plymouth, and London. Thomas had no children, and on his death in 1792, the Fowelscombe estate was left to his three brothers. Two months later, Fowelscombe was offered to let:

> *March 1792. FOWELSCOMBE MANSION HOUSE to let and entered immediately, either with or without the furniture.*
>
> *Hall 24ft x 28ft. Drawing Room 26ft x 18ft. Eating room 20ft x 16ft. Small breakfast parlour with suitable lodging rooms, a exceedingly good kitchen where there is a very good smoke-jack, a dairy, pantry, cellar, brewhouse. Excellent water brought in pipes in never failing spring, poultry yard, 2 stables, 2 large walled gardens with 2 terraces. extensive lawn of 50 acres.*
>
> *Also to let 3 years, Barton of Fowelscombe also of 7 or 14 years, 100 acres of good arable, Fowelscombe or Witchcombe, together with freehold 2 barns etc.*
>
> *Further particulars from John King, Plymouth, Robert King, Dean Prior, or Richard King, Hays Wharf, Tooley Street, London.*
>
> *Also to be sold – Livestock. Ewes and lambs, 50 fat wethers, 100 hoggets, several rams, 4 milch cows, 4 ditto with calves, 9 steers, 3 yearlings, 4 hackney horses, 4 draught horses, 6 pall horses, 4 colts 2 breed mares with foals. Part of estate of Fowelscombe.*

This describes a simple manor house of the period with three large chambers on the ground floor and little else of note. It was probably somewhat neglected and old-fashioned, having been occupied for many years by an ageing old bachelor. The smoke-jack in the kitchen might even have been there since the house was built. Whatever its condition, Fowelscombe obviously did not appeal to Thomas King's brothers. John, the eldest brother, died in 1795, and Robert and Richard decided to do a swap. By indentures of release dated July 1807, Robert traded his interest in Fowelscombe to Richard, who gave the manor of North Huish, which he had purchased in 1786, in return. The Kings had built a house for themselves next to the church at North Huish, not far from the grand new house that William Fowell built at Black Hall in 1600. Both houses survive. Robert was the only brother to have any children, and he had six sons. The eldest was John King, who inherited Fowelscombe from his uncle in 1811.

It would seem that Fowelscombe had sunk in status in the eyes of its owners. It was no longer their

Tythe Survey map

principal seat – far from it. The manor was at Ludbrook, outside Ugborough and Fowelscombe was listed as a farm, a fate which overtook many such small manor-houses. For most the decline continued, with cattle in the parlour and poultry roosting everywhere. But Fowelscombe had a reprieve, although sadly only temporary as far as its final end was concerned.

Only a year after inheriting Fowelscombe from his uncle, John's father died. It may be that Fowelscombe was let but in that year John King bought himself a property on the southern edge of Dartmoor, called Hayford. It was relatively small, and it would seem that his idea was to turn this into a hunting lodge. He was master of the South Devon hunt and must have considered Fowelscombe too far from the moor. From then on he spent lavishly on Hayford, turning it into a gentleman's residence of some distinction. It is not known how much time or money he spent at Fowelscombe. What does seem certain is that John King, like so many before and since, found that large properties and extensive building programmes run away with far more money than was ever anticipated.

At this point a gentleman by the name of Servington Savery entered the scene. The Savery's were a family of similar origins and history to the Fowells, their fortunes made in the legal profession, and living at this time in a manorhouse at Shilstone, near Modbury. Servington Savery was a solicitor and Collector of Crown Rents and presumably looked after the affairs of John King. He lent him money, accepting the Fowelscombe estate as surety. And in 1838 he foreclosed on John King who owed him almost £10,000. Thereafter we find him in possession of both Fowelscombe and Hayford.

In that year, *The Exeter & Plymouth Gazette* reported that Servington Savery of Modbury

purchased of John King the Fowelscombe estate. We hear that it is a splendid property and that it is immediately to undergo a thorough repair so as to make it adapted for the residence of a true old English gentleman who keeps in prime style his pack of merry harriers, who enjoys to see his friends around his board and his tenantry and cottages prosperous under him. It is supposed that Mr Savery will occupy the house as soon as it is fit to receive him.

Savery also spent money on Hayford, extending it considerably, and adorned the walls with the Savery coat of arms.

It is interesting to discover that the two families were connected by marriage. Florence Fowell, daughter of the first Sir Edmond, married Servington Savery of Shilstone. She had no children, but this second Servington was a direct descendant of her husband by his first wife. Thomas King of North Huish also married a Savery.

Few houses have had such a complicated and intertwined history as Fowelscombe. Researching proved time-consuming and detective instincts were very necessary. Ferreting around North Huish, whose church was about to be made redundant and even sold off, a chance encounter led to a James Savery King, of Florida, USA. There is nothing like a keen American researching his ancestors for getting to the bottom of things. Long after this chapter was finished a weighty package arrived on the doorstep containing page upon page of information on the King and Savery families. My American was more interested in the families than the houses, but he had spent hours following up the various wills and lawsuits involved. Of the complex actions that resulted in Servington Savery first gaining, then losing, the two estates, he has this to say:

Fowelscombe was sold to Servington Savery by John King on 21 and 22 March, 1839 by deeds of Lease and Release. Servington Savery was the King family solicitor, or one of them, I should say. Certainly doing business with John King. John King owed Servington Savery almost £10,000 at this time for legal services and loans,

Exactly what the pressures were, is unknown and I had heard two stories. One that John King was in bad shape financially and the other that Servington Savery was in bad financial shape later when the estate returned to the Kings. In reality, neither is true. John did indeed owe the money but prior to this he bought The Grove in Hampshire which is a magnificent estate. It is now known as Exton Cottage.

In any event, John King pursuaded his son, Richard to sign his inheritance away when he reached the age of 21 years. With this, Fowelscombe was sold for £23,700, a profit of some £13,700. In today's money this is about a $239,750 profit. It is quite obviously a tidy sum. Servington Savery was also a wealthy man and in the ensuing lawsuit, it is stated at the end that neither party is to be tainted by the legal action. I have an original letter given to me by Robert Savery from John Thomas Savery to his grandfather, Christopher Savery wherein he mentions Fowelscombe and the improvements that Servington Savery is making and almost finished with. The letter is dated December 21, 1839 and is one of my proud possessions. The John Thomas Savery mentioned above was the only brother to my great grandmother, Frances (Savery) King.

The decree from the House of Lords is dated 'Friday 9th May, 1856' and returns Fowelscombe to John King and restores the inheritance rights to his son, Richard King. The original Bill was filed by Richard King in March 1847 but took this long to get as far as the House of Lords. There were legal 'logjams' even then!

John King died 'in the saddle' on Brent Moor (Dartmoor) on 19 February, 1861 at the age of 73 while hunting the elusive fox with Squire Trelawny's hounds. I have his death certificate. He was buried in a large tomb on the immediate Southeast corner of Ugborough Church. The face side had fallen over many years ago and I had it repaired. It was sound and rigid in September of 1977 when I was there. A wrought iron fence has long since rusted away but the tomb is in good shape.

John King's family all remained in Hampshire and the male issue died out.

White's Directory for 1850 states that Fowelscombe was the seat of Servington Savery, and that it was a fine mansion in the Tudor style.

The mansion has been enlarged in modern times and contains many large and elegant apartments. Its grounds are extensive and tastefully laid out and command charming views.

This would indicate that it was Savery who enlarged the house. He lived there with his wife Mary and two daughters – and ten servants. He, also, kept his hounds there. Later he is recorded as living in Plymouth at the home of Mrs Caroline Lewis, and it was there that he died in 1856. His will has not been traced, but in that same year John King was once again in possession of Fowlescombe, but not of Hayford which remained the property of Mary Savery.

Given that the Kings began proceedings for the recovery of their property in 1847, Savery would have stopped spending anything on Fowelscombe, and may even have abandoned it altogether.

Some records state that Savery removed panelling and the staircase from Fowelscombe and incorporated them at Hayford. If this was the case, then they no longer exist, and no records of them at Hayford have come to light. What was moved was the large clock that once graced the entrance tower at Fowelscombe.

Built in 1810, one year before the death of Thomas King, it was commissioned from Samuel Northcote, one of the foremost clockmakers of his day, living in Plymouth. He had been apprenticed to Thomas Mudge in London (whose family had lived at Hayford many generations earlier).

Hayford Hall, resplendent with the clock from Fowelscombe; 1969 sales particulars

Turret clocks are rare, and the Fowelscombe clock is the only one that Samuel Northcote is known to have made. A massive cast iron frame is required to support the mechanism, making them large and cumbersome, with the weights suspended, being some 25 feet long. The exact date of its removal to Hayford Hall is not known, but the resemblance between the two towers is striking – indeed, the front of Hayford Hall seems to be an attempt to recreate Fowelscombe on the slopes of Dartmoor.

The frame is cast-iron, and the corner pillars have knob finials, the ends of the frame being cast in one piece and the front and back rails nutted through the posts.

All the wheels are brass, with six crossings, and the pivots run in turned brass bushes. The wooden barrels have been fitted with steel strips to protect them from damage when the weight-lines, originally ropes, were replaced by wire. The clock probably ran for at least four days on a winding, perhaps a week.

The going train has four wheels including the scape-wheel, and an achor escapement, with Harrison's maintaining power on the 2nd wheel arbor. The pendulum has a lead lenticular bob and a flat iron rod with a slot for the pin on the pendulum crutch. The train leads off through a friction drive to a centre arbor which has the motion-work on the back and the setting dial and striking rack at the front. From the motion-work there is a minute rod and a disc with two rods to the hour hand.

The setting-dial has three wheels and a fly, the lifting-pins for the hammer being on the 2nd wheel; there is rack striking.

The setting dial is inscribed 'Samuel Northcote, Plymouth 1810'. This would be Samuel Northcote II, the brother of the painter. (Revd. J. G. M. Scott)

John King died in 1861, and in 1865, Fowelscombe and 410 acres were put up for sale. Richard King can never have regarded it as his home, and lived at Exton, Hants, where he died in 1888. The details of the 'Mansion House' are brief in the extreme, simply listing an entrance hall, Dining Room and Drawing Room, Library, Bedrooms, 3 Dressing Rooms, 5 attics, servants hall, kitchens, parlour etc. walled garden, hot houses etc.

No hint is given as to the condition of the house, but sale catalogues of that period were usually eulogistic in their descriptions, giving great details of room sizes and their fittings etc. It may be that John King returned to a rundown property, already partially derelict.

It is not known whether Fowelscombe found a purchaser at this time, but it seems unlikely as the next reference, in 1890, is that Fowelscombe belonged to the Reverend Gordon Walters* who had married a Miss King, one of Richard's three daughters Apparently he never lived in the house, which thereafter became a complete ruin.

c1907. The house is obviously derelict, but there are fragments of glass in the mullion window although the others are boarded up. The front door stands open – and there is nothing to indicate whether this was a family gathering, or a party of interested historians

The final act came in 1919 when the property was again placed on the market. The vendors were Lt Col Gerard Frederick Towlerton Leather, Captain Percival Charles du Sautoy Leather, Miss Alice Jane King and Miss Edith Marion King, daughters of Richard. The Towlerton Leathers were brothers, sons of Frederick John Leather of Middleton Hall in Northumberland, who married in 1863 Sophia Walters, the daughter of the Rev Charles Walters, vicar of Wardington in Oxfordshire – and presumably related to the Rev Gordon Walters. It was stated that "the title shall commence with a mortgage in fee for £12,000 made by an indenture dated 20th July, 1846 which after diverse transferees has been lately transferred to the vendors who sell as sole transferees".

The date of the mortgage is interesting, as Savery was then the owner of Fowelscombe.

---

*James S King of Florida gives his name as Rev John Vodin Walters.

c1907. The hall fireplace, which still exists, and the panelling, which does not

The auction date was 13th May, when "the old castellated mansion of Fowelscombe, with its walled gardens, pleasure grounds, stabling and two lodges, and two productive farms of Bolterscombe and Witchcombe" would be offered for sale.

The auctioneer does point out that "the Mansion, which unfortunately is now out of repair but occupies a most sheltered position, is capable of being repaired to its original importance. Its spacious pleasure grounds and terraces, walled fruit and vegetable gardens, courtyard and stabling is approached by an imposing avenue drive…"

It was the farms that sold, and the empty house went with Bolterscombe to Mr Nicholls, and later to the family that still owns it.

It would seem that the auctioneers were more than a little optimistic in their claim that the house was still capable of being restored. The process of decay had been going on at least since 1887, although a correspondent of *The Western Morning News* in 1925 reported that it had been in a fair condition in 1898, when he made a sketch of the granite fireplace dated 1537.

By 1903 it was completely unsafe. Two letters printed in *Country Life* magazine in November, 1952, record its final days:

The pleasure grounds have disappeared and the walled gardens are a sea of brambles, but there is still surviving in the woods a little way from the house a collection of buildings referred to as the Kennels. This little settlement appears to have gone unremarked but, lying well hidden, is a little piece of industrial history of which surely some records must exist? Situated on what appears to be an earth-mound, are the 'Kennels'. A curving wall, only twelve inches or so thick and around ten feet in height, encloses a large area, the only entrance to which is a narrow opening with two arrow slits low down on either side. Inside is a small building of no obvious purpose. At the far end are three cottages in an advanced stage of decay. They were of the simplest two up, two down design, but there is still clear evidence of their layout and function. Each cottage had a large fireplace and in two, clome ovens and hearths still exist. Some of the lath and plaster adheres to the walls – along with sycamores and ivy, and the line of the stairs to the upper floor is clear. Nettles abound, inside and out; these were quite obviously human habitations.

THE DESERTION OF A HOUSE

Sir,—I wonder if any of your readers can explain how Fowelscombe, in South Devon, came to be deserted in the middle of the 19th century (N. Pevsner, *Buildings of South Devon*, 1952).

I enclose a photograph of Fowelscombe taken recently. As can be seen, the outer walls (in front) are still sound, though the inside has largely fallen in and is very overgrown. I could find no signs of fire.

The 1946 ordnance map continues to show as at least a fenced drive what is now in fact nothing more than ruts in a field, as can just be seen on the left of the photograph.

Pevsner describes Fowelscombe as the "large mansion of the Fowel family"; but possibly the last owners were the Kings, to one of whose name there is a tomb of 1861 in near-by Ugborough churchyard, east of the chancel.—E. P. WARNER, *Guards' Club*, 16, *Charles Street*, W.1.

THE RUINED REMAINS OF FOWELSCOMBE, IN SOUTH DEVON
See letter: The Desertion of a House

Country Life, *October 3rd, 1952*

THE DESERTION OF A HOUSE

Sir,—My attention has been drawn to the letter about Fowelscombe, Devon, in your issue of October 3, and I think it may be of interest to recall my visit there more than 50 years ago. We went twice, I think in 1899 and again in 1903, and the first time we wandered all over the house. We came into the hall, with the large granite mullioned window shown in the photograph I send, and a large granite chimney-piece with the date 1537 and the initials T.F. and M.F. On the right was a partly panelled room with another granite chimney-piece, and behind that room was a wide oak staircase. At the end of the house shown in the photograph were what must have been a charming drawing-room and a door leading to the garden.

Upstairs we found a small closet leading out of one of the bedrooms which had many little shelves—perhaps a powder closet. On the second visit, in 1903 we did not dare to venture up the stairs.

We were told afterwards that W. H. Smith had thought of buying and restoring the house, but the dry rot was found to be too far advanced. The carved oak had been sold in 1887. When the house had become quite unsafe, cattle had wandered in and there was danger of accidents, the roof was taken off and all the interior pulled down. The large mullioned window and others, the two stone chimney-pieces and two granite arched doorways were then bought by the late Mr. Philip Champernowne and built into his house, Beckhams, at Manaton.

Margaret Champernowne, mentioned in the letter of October 24, lived there during her widowhood and died in 1730, when it came to her third son, Henry, and it was after his death in 1757 that it was sold.— C. E. CHAMPERNOWNE (MISS), 252c, *Kew Road, Richmond, Surrey*.

FOWELSCOMBE, DEVON, ABOUT FIFTY YEARS AGO
See letter: The Desertion of a House

Country Life, *November 21st, 1952*

A fourth cottage completes the row, outside the compound wall and of somewhat larger and superior quality, perhaps the home of the overseer. To the rear of the cottages, which have no windows on this side, only the entrance doors, the ground falls very steeply to a pond formed by damming the stream. The track continues around the hillside, through the trees, and the purpose of the cottages suddenly becomes apparent. The hillside is honeycomed with quarries. Some stretch back for a considerable distance although now overgrown and derelict for many, many years. The track eventually leads down to the pond and examination of the dam shows that it was once a substanial affair with sluice gates, and could have held back a large volume of water. All this has long since fallen into disrepair and the water seeps through where it will, feeding the stream that runs down the valley.

The kennel cottages, 1997

Looking back upwards, the hill seems unnaturally steep, and the layout begins to make sense as the quarries are all off the track that circles round the pond. Walking away from the 'kennels' with these discoveries fresh in the mind, the track that leads out of the woods takes on a greater significance. It is well worn, and wide, and climbs at an easy angle, bordered on the side that slopes downwards by several large and mature beech trees. All of them have a remarkably straight trunk on the inner side and are free of branches for a considerable height overhanging the track. Closer examination reveals scars on the trunks all at the same height as if a rope had been wound tightly round them – perhaps to haul sledges uphill. Even the two fallen beeches bear these marks. From the top of the fields the track disappears. It may have continued over the hill to the house, or it may have gone down to the lower lodge. The whole valley would appear to have been a rich source of building stone, for there is evidence of smaller quarries along the drive from the west front that leads uphill towards the 'kennels', although these may have been the source of building material for the house itself.

These would be the buildings referred to as the 'Kennel Yard' etc in the 1919 particulars, and either John King or Servington Savery must have adapted the former quarry cottages to house their hounds.

Memories are vague, and accounts conflict. It is all so long ago, over a century, since there was any life in the old house. It is difficult to accurately trace the sequence of ownership that led to Fowelscombe being abandoned – and ultimately to its dereliction and decay. Now very few even remember it and soon it will be just a mention on the maps in medieval writing to mark the site of an once historic house.

Sources

Survey of Hayford House, Mrs P Whiteway.
MSS of James Savery King.
West Devon Record Office 712/1/8.